MORE
Reignite Your Purpose.
THAN A
Rediscover Joy at Work.
MOTTO

JUSTIN ROBBINS

MetricSherpa

Copyright © 2026 Metric Sherpa, Inc
All rights reserved

No part of this publication may be reproduced, stored in or introduced into a retrieval system, or transmitted, in any form, or by any means (electronic, mechanical, photocopying, recording, or otherwise), without the prior permission of the publisher. Direct permission requests to permissions@metricsherpa.com.

Justin Robbins is available for your next live or virtual event. For more information or to book an event, email speaking@justinmrobbins.com or visit justinmrobbins.com.

Cover and interior design:
Marty Shaughnessy, Deklanmedia
Cover image © 24DIY / Adobe Stock

ISBN 979-8-9946993-0-0 (Paperback)
ISBN 979-8-9946993-1-7 (Digital)

Library of Congress Control Number: 2026901906

Printed in the United States of America

For Marie, Peyton, Carter, Oliver, and Emersyn.

Thank you for cheering on the crazy ideas, trusting the big leaps, and choosing the adventure every time.

This work exists because you made the risk worth taking.

TABLE OF CONTENTS

INTRODUCTION   xi
When Words Stop Working

CHAPTER 1   1
The Chasm Between Our Words and Our Actions

CHAPTER 2   9
The Reason Motivation Fails Leaders

CHAPTER 3   17
Purpose Needs a Rhythm

CHAPTER 4   25
Clarity. Making Meaning Visible in Daily Work

CHAPTER 5   33
Intentionality. Enable Standards to Hold Under Pressure

CHAPTER 6   41
Connection. Why Belonging Sustains Effort

CHAPTER 7   49
Recovery. Designing Work That Restores Energy

CHAPTER 8   57
The Leader's Role in Making Purpose Real

CHAPTER 9   83
Measuring What Work Actually Feels Like

CHAPTER 10   99
Turning the Words Into the Work

CONCLUSION: THE PROMISE THAT REPLACED THE SMILE   105

APPENDIX

RHYTHM Operating System	109
Why Satisfaction Is Not Engagement	111
A Manager's Reference: Staying Connected	115
Mechanism Case Study: Legacy Checks	121
The First 90 Days	124
Rating Scales Explained	135
Purpose Reality Check	136
What Breaks First Trade-Off Map	140
Reinforcement Audit	145
Contribution Visibility Map	150
Completion Integrity Check	154
Effort Concentration Heatmap	158
Cadence Builder	162

ENDNOTES   169

INDEX   171

INTRODUCTION
When Words Stop Working

Growing up, my family loved diners. The kind with cracked vinyl booths, servers who called you "honey," and menus so big they barely fit on the table. One diner we visited had a motto printed on the front door: "Service with a Smile." And sure enough, the server smiled when she greeted our table.

But when my mom asked for extra syrup, the smile faded. When the kitchen got my order wrong, it turned into a sigh. When the check came, the smile was optional.

Even as a kid, I thought: if this is service with a smile, I'd hate to see service without one.

That moment stuck with me. The problem was not the smile. The problem was that the promises stayed as words.

Organizations love mottos; inspiring slogans are everywhere.

People First.

Customer Obsessed.

We Make Life Better.

Writing mottos is easy. Living them is hard.

I advised a company proud of "We put people first." It was everywhere—posters, onboarding, presentations. Yet employees described long hours, missed family time, and leaders who listened only sometimes. The slogan existed, but it wasn't put into practice.

> This gap is where trust is lost, energy drains, and meaningful work fades. When language doesn't guide decisions, culture suffers.

You cannot train culture in orientation or expect values on a wall to change behavior. Culture emerges from what is prioritized, rewarded, ignored, and excused each day. The organizations that last turn mottos into action. Promises are only credible when they shape daily reality. Brand promises break when leaders don't make purpose tangible in day-to-day work.

This book focuses on closing the gap between words and practice. Not through speeches or new programs, but through rhythms that make purpose part of daily experience.

A rhythm is the repeatable pattern of decisions, behaviors, and signals that work reinforces every day, whether leaders intend it or not. When purpose becomes practice, clarity returns, effort is sustainable, and meaning is real.

When Work Teaches People to Settle

The loss of purpose rarely announces itself. It does not arrive as a resignation letter or a dramatic career pivot. It shows up quietly. Through small compromises that feel reasonable in the moment. Through systems that reward output over judgment and endurance over intention. Most people do not abandon their ambition. They adapt to their environment.

They learn to be grateful, but not daring. Productive, but not passionate. Reliable, but restrained. Not because they lack drive, but because the system teaches them what is realistic, safe, and will not create friction.

Over time, people stop investing discretionary energy. They narrow their focus. They do precisely what the work requires and little more. What looks like disengagement is often learned self-preservation.

I don't believe this is a problem of people's mindsets. It is a problem with the rhythms we've allowed to take root in our organizations.

• • •

When work lacks clear priorities, people guess.
When decisions feel arbitrary, people disengage.
When connection weakens, trust erodes.
When recovery disappears, energy collapses.

• • •

The result is drift. Not failure. Drift. And drift is predictable.

The Operating System Behind Purpose

Most leaders are not indifferent to this problem.

They respond, step in, correct, reinforce, and re-explain. For a moment, things improve. Then pressure returns, attention shifts, and behavior reverts. That cycle reveals the real issue.

Purpose collapses when it depends on leaders intervening at the right moments rather than on work reinforcing the right patterns all the time.

When belief requires constant effort to sustain, it eventually exhausts those who carry it. That is the point where intention must give way to design. That requires an operating system.

The RHYTHM Operating System names the leadership roles that must be structurally reinforced to ensure purpose endures. These jobs do not function as isolated actions or personal habits. Without structure, leaders carry them manually. With structure, the work carries them. That shift from intervention to design marks the point where purpose stops depending on heroics.

RHYTHM stands for:

Resolve What Matters (Clarity)
Leaders decide what truly matters, why it matters, and what does not. Ambiguity drains energy faster than workload.

Hold the Line (Intentionality)
Leaders protect priorities under pressure. Trade-offs stay visible. Values hold when decisions get hard.

You Belong Here (Connection)
Work makes effort visible and meaningful. People experience relevance, not replaceability.

Tempo the Work (Recovery)
Leaders pace demand so excellence remains sustainable rather than extractive.

Hear the System (Measurement)
Leaders measure what work actually feels like, not just what it produces.

Make It Repeat (Cadence)
Purpose embeds through rhythm, not reminders. What matters shows up again and again.

How This Book Is Designed

This book moves from diagnosis to design.

The opening chapters examine why purpose breaks under pressure and why efforts to motivate consistently disappoint leaders who care. From there, the book introduces purpose as a rhythm rather than a statement. Purpose holds when it is repeated in how work gets done.

The core of the book explores the four foundational rhythms of purposeful work: clarity, intentionality, connection, and recovery. Each chapter focuses on the leadership decisions that either reinforce or undermine them. The final chapters turn to leadership responsibility. How leaders measure what work actually feels like. How they translate a motto into daily experience. How they stop carrying the burden of purpose alone and instead build systems that sustain it.

This book argues that leaders should design work that reinforces purpose through rhythm, so people stop conserving energy and start investing it.

That is how words begin to work again.

"Gutta cavat lapidem non vi, sed saepe cadendo."
A water drop hollows a stone, not by force, but by falling often.

— Ovid

CHAPTER 1

The Chasm Between Our Words and Our Actions

The Slow Erosion of Meaning

Work rarely becomes meaningless overnight. It loses meaning gradually, through a series of small moments in which effort no longer lines up with impact. People do what is asked, but they no longer understand why it matters. Where clarity fades first, long before motivation does.

People want to do good work. But when priorities shift without explanation, decisions seem inconsistent, or values no longer guide daily choices, confidence erodes. People guess, hesitate, and become quietly compliant. Work moves from meaningful to survivable.

From the outside, everything can look fine: goals exist, values are documented, and leaders communicate. Yet inside, people spend more energy interpreting what matters than doing the work. This invisible cost of effort goes unnoticed by leaders.

Employees rarely say,

"The message doesn't match the experience."

Instead, they adapt, narrow focus, and stick to what feels safest.

Discretion replaces judgment, and initiative becomes mere execution. Apathy often signifies uncertainty, not indifference.

When people no longer believe clarity exists, they stop investing emotionally. They still show up and perform, but work loses purpose as its connection to meaning fades. This erosion is quiet. No dramatic breakdown, just a subtle shift in how people relate to work.

Through well-intentioned decisions, leaders have created workplaces where caring comes at unpredictable cost. People adapt by withdrawing. The responsibility now is not to rekindle belief, but to change the patterns that taught people to pull back.

The Leadership Blind Spot
Most leaders care deeply about their people and their organizations. They work long hours, carry actual pressure, and feel a genuine sense of responsibility for results. When misalignment appears, it rarely comes from indifference. It comes from an assumption.

Leaders assume intent translates. They assume clarity travels intact. They think people understand the meaning of their words and will therefore act on them consistently. From a leadership position, the logic behind decisions seems obvious. Priorities make sense because leaders see the whole picture. Context feels shared because it lives in their heads and conversations. But teams experience decisions downstream, stripped of explanation and nuance. What matters to teams is not what leaders intend, but what the work consistently demands. That translation happens through what gets measured, rewarded, escalated, or ignored. Over time, teams depend more on consistent system reinforcement than on words.

Early in my career, I learned this lesson the hard way. I became a people manager at a young age and immediately felt the need to prove myself. I wanted to earn credibility and be well-liked, and I believed extreme candor would help me do both. So I adopted a policy of transparency. I shared everything I could, including detailed performance metrics for my team.

One report seemed harmless. It listed multiple performance measures, but in the upper-left corner sat a metric showing time spent per customer. I shared the report openly, without guidance on how to interpret it. What I did not realize was that placement taught priority. Without my guidance, my team assumed the upper-left metric was most important. Though the value hadn't changed, behavior shifted: conversations shortened, people rushed, and service suffered. The system—not the principle—directed their actions.

A single metric, positioned without context, taught my team more about what mattered than any value statement ever could. At no point did I tell people to rush. I did not change expectations. But intent never stood a chance against what the system encouraged.

This is the leadership blind spot: Alignment is not about intention, but about what actually happens. The gap between what leaders say and what employees experience drives disengagement long before leaders see it.

What the Gap Feels Like on the Inside

The gap between words and experience doesn't announce itself; employees feel it. It shows as hesitation, second-guessing, and quiet pauses before decisions. When expectations feel unstable, work becomes less about doing right and more about avoiding mistakes. As clarity fades, effort intensifies.

People spend more time double-checking assumptions and seeking approval than making an impact. They work harder to protect themselves from misalignment than to create meaning. This is exhausting.

When work stops feeling coherent, people struggle to connect their effort to the outcome. Progress feels uneven. Wins feel temporary. Mistakes feel costly in ways that are hard to expect. Over time, people adjust.

People narrow their focus to what gets noticed, avoiding questions that slow things down. Initiative gives way to compliance—not for lack of ideas, but because being wrong seems riskier than being right. Leadership rarely sees these shifts immediately. Judgment dulls. Creativity wanes. Ownership shrinks. Effort loses reliability, so people pull back.

Work changes: conversations shorten, quality slips, and collaboration becomes transactional. People conserve energy rather than invest it. By the time leaders notice, the gap has already reshaped behavior.

Why Engagement Programs Miss the Mark

When leaders sense disengagement, their instinct is to act quickly. That instinct is understandable. Energy feels low. Feedback sounds flat. Results slip. So organizations respond with programs.

Engagement surveys. Recognition platforms. Wellness initiatives.

Listening sessions. Town halls. Despite good intentions, little actually changes.

That is not because these efforts are useless. It is because they aim at the surface while leaving the underlying conditions intact.

Engagement programs ask people how they feel. They do not change what people experience.

Part of the confusion stems from treating employee satisfaction and employee engagement as the same thing.

* * *

Satisfaction answers whether expectations are being met.
Pay. Hours. Benefits. Tools.

Engagement answers whether the work is worth investing in.
Purpose. Belonging. Impact.

* * *

Most engagement efforts try to address the second question without thoroughly examining the first, or they improve the basics while assuming meaning will follow. It rarely does.

In my work with leaders, I often walk teams through four questions every employee is trying to answer:

1. What do I get?
2. What can I give?
3. Do I belong?
4. How can we grow?

When the answers feel coherent, people invest. When they don't, people protect themselves. Engagement programs struggle because they operate alongside work rather than reshaping it.

Layers are added, but the mechanics that teach care are left unchanged. Over time, frustration grows. Each initiative raises hopes that the system can't support. When follow-through fails, people learn to lower expectations. The message is obvious, though unstated.

Talking about work is safer than changing it.

The Cost of the Gap

The gap between what organizations say and how work operates carries a cost. It isn't always obvious, but it happens consistently.

Decision-making slows—people hesitate, escalate, and seek permission. Work takes longer, not because of a lack of skill, but because of eroded clarity. With inconsistent expectations, people default to safety. Standards slip, rework increases, and pride diminishes.

Trust erodes next. Not a distrust in intentions, but in reliability. People stop believing their efforts will be consistently judged. Commitment becomes conditional. Performance data distorts. Activity replaces impact. Leaders see motion without momentum and wonder why results stall despite visible effort.

Turnover rises—some leave, others disengage. Institutional knowledge drains and hiring costs grow. Teams grow thinner as complexity increases. The brand is impacted last: broken employer promises show up in customer experience.

Over time, the system teaches people how much to invest and when to hold back. The actual cost of the gap shows up in what organizations lose quietly. Judgment weakens. Energy dissipates. Momentum has stalled. By the time leaders clearly see the impact, those losses have already compounded.

Purpose breaks down when leaders rely on motivation rather than on designing work that consistently reinforces it.

CHAPTER 2

The Reason Motivation Fails Leaders

Why Motivation Feels Like the Right Lever

Motivation is appealing because it is immediate. When energy dips, leaders feel it quickly. Meetings grow quieter. Initiative slows. Feedback flattens. Motivation offers a response that feels both human and fast. Say the right thing. Tell a good story. Rally the team. See the room transform. That responsiveness creates confidence. Leaders see a visible shift and reasonably conclude they've addressed the issue.

Motivation also aligns with how many leaders learned to lead. They were told presence builds influence. Inspiration provides direction. Belief drives momentum. These approaches work well in moments of change, crisis, or launch. They just do not last.

Motivation also keeps the problem close to people rather than embedded in the work itself. If performance slips, it feels simpler to re-energize a team than to reexamine priorities, workload, decision rights, or measures of success. Most leaders reach for the relational response first.

There is also a cultural bias at play. Organizations celebrate motivated people. They reward enthusiasm. They promote energy as a signal of commitment. Over time, motivation becomes shorthand for engagement, even when the work itself undermines sustained effort. This framing puts pressure in the wrong place.

When motivation becomes the primary solution, leaders compensate for inconsistency with intensity. They smooth friction with encouragement. They ask people to push through instead of asking whether the push is necessary. For a while, people may respond. Many want to help. They care about their teams and leaders. They apply discretionary effort to bridge the gap. That effort is costly.

Motivation works best as a spark, not a scaffold. It can trigger action, but it cannot hold weight. When the underlying structure remains unchanged, motivation eventually loses its ability to sustain effort. Temporary forces cannot maintain permanent demands.

> During an interview, a senior leader at a large financial services company shared with me a moment that reframed how they understood disengagement and burnout.
>
> Attrition had been climbing. Exit data pointed to familiar explanations. The work was intense. Expectations were high. People lacked resilience. The leadership team discussed motivation and stamina openly, yet the conclusions never settled. Something felt off. They began interviewing employees, and a pattern emerged quickly.

The offers had been honored. Pay arrived as promised. Hours matched what had been described. Benefits were intact. On paper, nothing had been broken. Yet employees described feeling misled, not about the role, but about their ability to perform it well.

One core system shaped nearly every interaction. It was slow, unstable, and dependent on workarounds. Long-tenured employees had adapted. New hires encountered it almost immediately. Tasks took longer than expected. Attention shifted from helping customers to managing risk. Progress became harder to sustain.

No one had mentioned it. Not during interviews. Not during onboarding. Not during training. The omission wasn't deliberate. The system had simply faded into the background of "how things work here."

Employees described the experience differently, but the meaning remained the same.

"I can't do my job the way I thought I would." "I spend more time compensating for the tools than serving customers." "I don't feel set up to succeed."

What began as workflow friction quickly eroded confidence. Capability felt constrained by the environment rather than supported by it.

Leaders reacted with care. They leaned in personally. Coaching increased. Encouragement followed, and conversations centered on mindset, perseverance, and effort. People's energy served as a buffer between

> expectations and reality.
>
> That was the lightbulb moment. Burnout wasn't emerging from long hours or weak resolve. It was forming in the gap between what leaders believed they were providing and what the work actually demanded. The work held together because people kept compensating for it. Motivation didn't fail. It was quietly consumed, keeping a fragile system upright.

The Limits of Motivation at Scale

Motivation works best in contained environments. Small teams. Short time horizons. Clear goals. Direct feedback. But the scale of things alters everything. As organizations grow, work fragments. Layers now spread decisions. Shared understanding thins. People operate farther from intent, with fewer anchors for judgment and more constraints to navigate. In those environments, motivation loses precision.

A message that energizes one team can confuse another. A rallying call that inspires action in one moment can create misalignment in the next. Without a consistent structure underneath, motivation amplifies whatever system already exists, including its flaws. This is where leaders often feel the disconnect between intentions and actions most sharply.

Their communication is clear. They show conviction. They see pockets of energy. Results remain uneven. Some teams surge while others stall. Progress feels episodic rather than cumulative. Motivation influences emotion faster than it influences direction. At scale, effort needs coordination more than intensity.

People need stable priorities, clear boundaries, and predictable decision logic. When those elements are missing, motivation fills the gap briefly before dissipating. Pressure speeds up the problem. As complexity increases, leaders rely on motivation to compensate for friction. They ask for flexibility. They praise resilience. Each ask feels reasonable on its own. Over time, those asks stack up. People absorb inconsistency as part of the job. They work around vague priorities. They compensate for process gaps—energy shifts from value creation to instability management. Motivation becomes a tax.

The more the system relies on it, the more effort it consumes just to keep work moving. Progress slows even as activity increases. When motivation becomes the stabilizer, the system is already unstable.

Effort Is Not the Same as Energy

Effort is visible. Energy is not. Leaders see effort in output. Tasks completed. Hours worked. Messages sent. From the outside, effort can look strong even when something underneath is failing.

Energy shows up differently. In judgment, initiative, and how people respond when something unexpected happens. Energy determines whether effort compounds or merely accumulates. The two are often confused.

In environments where motivation carries too much weight, effort rises as energy declines. People stay busy. They push through, but their thinking narrows. Decisions shrink, and risk tolerance decreases. While work technically gets done, authentic progress stalls.

Burnout often surprises leaders because effort never disappears. Many times, it intensifies. People compensate. They absorb friction. They stretch themselves to keep things moving. Energy drains quietly.

As energy declines, people stop extending judgment. They lean more heavily on rules. They escalate decisions they once handled independently. Certainty replaces initiative. This is not clearly visible on a dashboard. Output remains steady. Responsiveness stays high. This change concerns the application of effort. Effort without energy is brittle.

It lacks the capacity to absorb change. Under pressure, it cannot sustain quality. It cannot recover when demand spikes. Over time, the cost becomes visible. Decisions slow. Errors increase, and collaboration weakens. Work feels heavier, even when output remains high. The problem is the work's structure, not people's motivation.

Burnout Is a System Outcome, Not a Personal Failure

Burnout does not begin with exhaustion. It starts with sustained misalignment between effort and payoff. People give energy. They absorb friction. They compensate for instability. For a long time, they have managed.

Burnout sets in later, when that compensation becomes permanent. Most organizations treat burnout as an individual issue. Stress management. Mindfulness. Time-off reminders. Wellness programs designed to help people cope better. Those efforts offer relief. They do not address the cause.

Burnout emerges when people care for too long within systems that require constant compensation. When effort repeatedly stabilizes work instead of improving it, energy drains even among committed teams.

This is why burnout often affects top performers first. They stretch more. Fill in the gaps. Become reliable. Over time, that reliability turns into an expectation. Output continues. Investment does not. Recovery becomes optional. Boundaries erode. Burnout follows.

The warning signs are subtle.

It's decision fatigue, less tolerance for ambiguity, and a greater preference for certainty. At this stage, asking people to be more resilient misses the point. Indeed, resilience is essential. Recovery is undoubtedly necessary. Neither can compensate for an unstable design indefinitely.

Sustainable effort requires recovery built into how work operates.

It means clear priorities. It's a reasonable workload. And boundaries that allow energy to return. Without those elements, burnout becomes inevitable because the system keeps asking for compensation.

Why Sustained Effort Requires More Than Motivation

Motivation has a role. It starts movement. Helps to focus attention. Encourages teams to push through moments of change. Sustained effort asks for something else. Consistency. Coherence. Patterns people can rely on when energy fluctuates.

When leaders rely on motivation to stabilize performance, they place the burden of consistency on people rather than on the work. Over time, that burden becomes unsustainable.

Organizations experience cycles of urgency and exhaustion. Push periods followed by recovery attempts. Surges of effort followed by dips in energy. Motivation fuels the peaks. The system determines the valleys. Sustained effort depends on whether people can trust the work to hold steady.

When priorities remain clear, decisions follow logic, and effort leads to outcomes that make sense, motivation becomes additive. When those conditions do not exist, motivation becomes consumptive. It gets used up keeping things from falling apart. This is the distinction most leaders miss.

They focus on motivating people without ensuring the work can support sustained effort. They ask for more energy without redesigning the conditions that drain it. The result is predictable.

Effort continues—energy declines. Burnout spreads. Engagement fades quietly.

Motivation cannot close that gap. Closing it requires something more durable. Something repeatable. Something built into how work actually operates.

CHAPTER 3

Purpose Needs a Rhythm

Why Purpose Breaks Without Rhythm

Purpose does not fail all at once. It weakens when people cannot translate it into how work actually moves day-to-day. The intent exists, but the timing, pace, and expectations do not.

I learned this long before I worked in organizations. I discovered it as a percussionist.

One of a drummer's primary responsibilities is keeping tempo. In professional settings, musicians rely on a shared metronome or click track to stay aligned. It establishes pace, reduces guesswork, and allows each player to focus on their part while trusting the collective timing. When it works, coordination feels effortless. Once, it didn't.

> Mid-performance, the click track failed. The system that had kept everyone aligned disappeared, and it became my responsibility to maintain the tempo for the rest of the set. That responsibility involved more than staying

on beat. Pace mattered. Too fast or too slow, and the performance would unravel. Feel mattered too. A rock groove demands something different from a shuffle or a swing. Timing without context would have been just as disruptive as losing time entirely. The audience never noticed.

Preparation made the difference. Rehearsal. Shared understanding. A common sense of how the music moved. Alignment continued even when the system failed. I had lived the opposite outcome months earlier. In a similar situation, without a shared rhythm, everything collapsed. The musicians were capable. The intent was clear. Execution failed anyway. The difference was rhythm. Organizations experience the same breakdown under pressure.

When systems strain, priorities shift, or conditions change, the mechanisms that once coordinated work weaken. Skill remains. Effort continues. What erodes is the shared timing and understanding of how work should progress.

Without rhythm, people compensate. They hesitate. Rush when they should pause. Monitor each other more closely. Energy drains as people work harder just to stay aligned. In these environments, purpose struggles to hold because people lack a repeatable pattern they can rely on when conditions change.

Rhythm provides that pattern. It stabilizes effort. Maintains potential. And allows coordination to continue even when tools fail, or pressure rises.

Without rhythm, even competent teams fall out of time.

Rhythm Is How Humans Sustain Meaning

People are not built to renegotiate meaning constantly. They rely on pattern and repetition to conserve cognitive effort and stabilize expectations. When conditions repeat, people stop reinterpreting the environment and start acting with confidence. This is how humans navigate complexity without exhausting attention or judgment (Bargh and Chartrand 1999)[1]. Rhythm is not a preference. It is a cognitive requirement.

When work lacks rhythm, people expend unnecessary effort trying to interpret expectations. They scan for cues. They reconsider decisions they believed were settled. They hesitate, not because they lack commitment, but because the environment no longer feels predictable. Meaning becomes fragile because it requires constant confirmation. Rhythm removes that burden.

Predictable patterns help people orient themselves without having to rethink their priorities every day. People know what matters, how decisions are made, and where to invest effort without waiting for instruction. This is how meaning stabilizes. Consistency lowers the effort required to navigate complexity.

When patterns hold, people redirect energy away from vigilance and toward judgment, creativity, and problem-solving. Without rhythm, even a clearly stated purpose becomes difficult to sustain.

Agreement to a purpose does not guide behavior under pressure. Experience does. What people have lived through repeatedly shapes their actions more powerfully than what they have been told, especially when time is scarce or risk feels high. Rhythm turns intention into expectation. It teaches people what will happen if they act, decide, or speak up.

Over time, people stop watching for exceptions and start relying on the pattern. That reliance matters. When people trust the rhythm of work, they take appropriate risks. They invest discretionary effort because the environment feels coherent enough to support it. When rhythm is absent, people protect themselves. They default to what feels safest. Meaning dissipates as effort becomes transactional.

Motivation cannot replace rhythm. Motivation can focus attention briefly. Rhythm sustains direction over time.

Every Organization Has Rhythms. Most Are Accidental.
No organization operates without rhythm. Work already moves in patterns. Meetings recur. Decisions follow familiar paths. Feedback arrives on a schedule, or it does not. Crises trigger predictable responses. Silence does too. These patterns exist whether leaders acknowledge them or not. Through repetition, they teach people how the organization actually functions.

People learn faster from experience than from explanation. Faster than strategy decks. More convincingly than value statements. They know when decisions are made. What gets attention. What escalates. What fades. They learn how long approval takes and when speed suddenly matters. They understand when it is safe to raise concerns and when it is better to wait. This learning happens through repetition, not intention.

Accidental rhythms form through repeated responses to pressure, habit, and legacy processes. Once established, they become self-reinforcing patterns that shape behavior independently of formal design (Feldman and Pentland 2003)[2]. People adapt quickly. New hires absorb these rhythms early. Leaders benefit from their efficiency without always seeing their cost.

These unintentional rhythms shape the reality of most employees' efforts. When meetings end without decisions, preparation declines. When feedback only arrives after failure, people limit risk. When priorities shift weekly, people narrow their focus. When recovery only appears after exhaustion, people pace themselves defensively. Work continues. Output remains. What changes is how people invest themselves.

Accidental rhythms rarely align with stated purpose. They form around urgency, convenience, and survival rather than intention. Over time, they replace what leaders say matters with what the work reinforces. People do not resist the purpose. They adapt to the rhythm.

When Rhythm and Purpose Align, Work Stabilizes

When rhythm and purpose align, work feels different. Not easier. More stable. People spend less time interpreting expectations and more time applying judgment. Decisions require less escalation. Effort compounds rather than resetting. Aligned rhythms reduce volatility. Priorities feel clearer. Trade-offs follow a recognizable logic. Feedback arrives in expected ways. Recovery stops feeling exceptional.

As a result, effort stops swinging wildly in response to pressure. Energy lasts longer. People trust that their investment will lead to a predictable outcome. That trust changes how they show up. They plan for the future. Concerns are raised by them earlier. They take responsibility instead of narrowly executing tasks. Judgment improves because the environment supports it.

Motivation plays a different role here. It enhances momentum instead of compensating for instability. Aligned rhythms reduce burnout without directly targeting it. When people no longer compensate for inconsistency, energy returns naturally. Attention widens. Creativity comes back. The system carries a greater share of the load.

Leaders feel the difference. Fewer escalations. Fewer reversals. Less emotional labor is required to keep things moving. Progress becomes steadier. Outcomes become more reliable. Purpose holds because it is reinforced by how work moves, not how it is described.

The Four Rhythms That Make Purpose Livable
Rhythm becomes practical through repeatable patterns. Across organizations, four rhythms appear whenever purpose moves from language into lived experience. They are not new ideas. Their power comes from consistency. They do not operate independently. When one weakens, the others strain. When they align, effort stabilizes, and meaning holds.

>The first rhythm is *clarity.*
>People need to know what matters now and why.

>The second rhythm is *intentionality*.
>How we choose to act every day influences who we are much more than occasional words do.

The third rhythm is ***connection***.

Work sustains effort when people feel seen and part of something larger than their role.

The fourth rhythm is ***recovery***.

Sustained effort depends on energy returning inside the work, not after it.

These rhythms succeed because they respect reality. People cannot operate indefinitely on motivation. Belief follows experience. Consistency shapes behavior faster than intent. Together, these rhythms turn purpose into something people can feel, not just recite.

The chapters that follow explore each rhythm in depth. Not as ideals, but as deliberate operating patterns, leaders can design because purpose holds when it moves with rhythm.

CHAPTER 4

Clarity

Making Meaning Visible in Daily Work

Confusion Costs More Than Leaders Realize

Most leaders underestimate how expensive confusion really is. Its impact hides because work keeps moving. People show up. Activity stays visible. From the outside, progress appears intact. Underneath, efforts are fragmenting as people shift from action toward interpreting what matters in ambiguous environments (Weick 1995)[3].

When priorities feel unclear, people hesitate. They seek confirmation. They minimize exposure. People delay decisions to avoid choices that others might question later. That uncertainty carries a cost.

They redirect energy from contribution towards interpretation. People spend effort decoding expectations instead of advancing the work. Over time, confidence erodes as judgment feels less supported. Confusion often precedes disengagement.

Leaders rarely create confusion intentionally. It emerges through growth, change, competing demands, and attempts to keep options open. The effect remains the same. When people cannot tell what matters most, effort loses direction.

One question immediately surfaces the existence of confusion:

> ***How will you know it when you see it?*** (purpose, success, misalignment, etc.)

When clarity exists, people answer confidently. They recognize progress, quality, and success without waiting for approval. When clarity is missing, answers vary. They depend on who you ask, when you ask, or what happened most recently. Work feels reactive rather than intentional.

Leaders often respond by communicating more. More updates. More context. More explanation. Volume does not resolve confusion when prioritization is missing. Clarity does not come from saying more. It comes from making meaning observable.

Clarity Is Not More Information

When leaders sense confusion, their instinct is to inform. They add background, explain intent, and hold more meetings. Each step feels responsible, but it's often just confusion that increases. That happens because information expands the field. Clarity narrows it.

Explaining everything leaves nothing that stands out. When every priority is mentioned, none feels decisive. People leave informed but still uncertain about what to attend to first. This is where good leadership creates friction.

Leaders believe clarity improves with context. In reality, clarity improves for teams when there are fewer variables. More information requires more interpretation. More interpretation leads to increased hesitation. Hesitation slows work and drains energy. Clarity works in the opposite direction.

It reduces choice. Clarity makes trade-offs visible. It defines what matters now and what can wait without penalty. Most work does not fail from a lack of understanding. It falters when people cannot prioritize competing demands.

Clarity addresses the questions that information leaves unanswered.

> *What takes precedence when priorities collide?*
> *What does good look like under pressure?*
> *When time is scarce, what should we safeguard?*

When those answers remain implicit, people fill the gaps themselves. Here is where alignment fractures and work fragments occur. Clarity requires leaders to choose. That choice creates focus. Focus creates movement.

What the Work Rewards Becomes the Definition of Clarity

People do not rely on statements to understand priorities. They rely on experience. Over time, work teaches people what matters by how it responds to effort.

What draws attention? What brings about a reward? What creates a sense of urgency? What disappears without consequence?

These patterns define success.

Leaders don't provide clarity by simply saying something. Their teams achieve clarity through reinforcement. When those align, effort stabilizes. When they diverge, confusion returns; regardless of the messaging, this is where clarity breaks down most often.

Organizations declare focus, then reward speed. They promote quality, then escalate volume. They encourage ownership, then override decisions under pressure. None of these choices is malicious. Most feel reasonable in isolation. Together, they create competing definitions of success.

People respond by following what works. They adapt to what moves fastest, avoid friction, or earn recognition. Over time, those adaptations harden into habits. Clarity shifts away from what leaders say matters and toward what the system validates. Therefore, clarity cannot survive through communication alone.

* * *

Metrics beat messages.
Incentives outlast intent.
Patterns teach faster than plans.

* * *

The work always resolves ambiguity. It teaches people which behaviors are safe, visible, and repeatable, especially during trade-offs.

When time runs short, what gives way? As resources tighten, what gets protected? If results disappoint, what gets challenged and what gets excused?

These moments define clarity more than any planning session ever could. Consistency strengthens clarity. It's when success looks the same across metrics, feedback, recognition, and decisions, when people can predict evaluation before acting, when expectations hold long enough to be trusted.

Clarity breaks down without that consistency. People stop relying on judgment and start relying on precedent. They repeat what worked last time, even when it no longer fits. Leaders often misread this as resistance when it actually reflects adaptation.

Decision Clarity Restores Energy

Decision boundaries shape how energy moves through work. When ownership is unclear, decision-making slows. People carry the risk personally. They replay outcomes. They wait for cues. Progress continues, but effort multiplies. That effort drains energy quietly. Decision clarity removes that burden.

When people know which decisions they own, which require collaboration, and which belong elsewhere, work moves more smoothly.

Judgment sharpens because accountability exists before pressure arrives. Leaders sometimes fear that more precise boundaries reduce flexibility. They usually increase it. Explicit ownership encourages initiative. Issues surface earlier. Decisions improve when expectations are set in advance rather than negotiated after the fact.

Decision clarity also protects leaders. Without boundaries, leaders become default escalation points. Their attention fragments across decisions that should never compete for it, and their capacity for more meaningful work shrinks.

When people trust the consistency of the message and feel clear and confident in the means of achieving it, they invest more fully. They stop conserving effort against second-guessing. They focus on outcomes rather than optics. The removal of ambiguity stabilizes employee efforts and eases strained leaders.

Clarity Holds When It Repeats

People lose clarity when they revisit it occasionally rather than reinforcing it through daily work. As a mentor once told me, "vision leaks". In other words, a priority set once does not remain clear indefinitely. Work shifts. Pressure reshapes urgency. Without reinforcement, focus erodes.

Clarity must operate as a rhythm. Not a quarterly message. Not a planning slide. A pattern people experience repeatedly. Leaders who sustain clarity recalibrate it as conditions change.

Early on, clarity orients. What matters? How success shows up. As work settles, clarity directs execution. What wins this week? What can wait? At milestones, clarity becomes reflective. What to continue. What to change. Where growth now lives.

These shifts matter. Asking the same questions in different moments weakens clarity. Adjusting focus to match where people are strengthens it.

The anchor question remains: *How will you know it when you see it?* That question keeps clarity grounded in observation rather than intention.

It reinforces priorities through repetition, not reminders.

None of this happens because people suddenly care more. It occurs because the work gives caring a structure that makes sense. When clarity repeats, people stop scanning for hidden priorities. They act with confidence because the environment supports judgment. Over time, clarity becomes something people feel, not debate. That stability allows intentionality to take root.

CHAPTER 5
Intentionality
Enable Standards to Hold Under Pressure

Identity Forms Through Repetition

Organizations do not become what they say they value. They become what they reinforce consistently (Schein 2017)[4]. Identity forms through repetition. What happens once creates memory. What happens repeatedly creates belief. Over time, people stop listening for intent and start trusting patterns.

So clarity alone is not enough. Clarity tells people what matters. Intentionality determines whether that message holds under pressure. Without repetition, even the clearest priorities remain fragile. They rely on memory, goodwill, and frequent reinforcement from leaders. That does not scale. People learn identity by watching what survives.

What priorities remain when trade-offs are made? Which behaviors receive reinforcement when shortcuts would be easier to take? Which standards remain intact when inconvenience appears?

These experiences accumulate. They teach people what the organization actually stands for. Over time, that learning becomes automatic.

People stop asking what matters and start acting as if they already know.

This is how culture forms. Through exposure. Small actions outweigh dramatic ones. A consistent response carries more weight than an occasional speech. A predictable decision builds more trust than a powerful message delivered once. It's for this reason that inconsistency carries such a high cost.

When reinforcement varies, people stay alert. They watch closely. They wait to see which version of the organization will show up. Their energy changes from contribution to vigilance. Intentionality removes that uncertainty. It creates stability by making reinforcement reliable. People know what to expect because they have experienced it repeatedly. Over time, identity stops feeling fragile and becomes established.

Intentionality depends on consistency, not perfection. Organizations do not need leaders who get it right every time. They need leaders who reinforce the same priorities often enough that people can rely on them. Clarity establishes direction. Intentionality makes that direction durable.

The Hidden Power of Everyday Trade-offs

Values become visible when priorities collide. Every day, leaders make decisions that favor one priority over another. Time gets allocated. Resources shift. Attention moves. In those moments, values move from abstract to observable. People notice because trade-offs remove ambiguity. They clarify what matters when everything cannot win. When leaders make those choices deliberately, intentionality becomes visible. When they avoid them, people fill the gaps themselves. Silence during trade-offs teaches as much as action.

When leaders do not intervene, people infer that they have permission. When decisions drift without explanation, teams assume priorities have changed. Over time, those assumptions harden into behavior. Leaders often underestimate how frequently these moments occur. They think of values as something reinforced periodically. Teams experience them as constant. A single decision rarely defines identity. Repeated trade-offs do.

When the same priorities win consistently, people stop questioning them. They organize efforts around what they know will hold. Judgment improves because expectations feel stable. When trade-offs vary, people hedge. They wait for cues. Effort shifts away from ownership and toward self-protection. Intentionality lives in these ordinary decisions. Over time, these choices accumulate. They form a pattern that people rely on or work around. Either way, identity emerges.

> I'm an early bird, and when I travel, I look for excellent breakfast places. On a work trip to Mason, Ohio, I found the Half Day Cafe. The reviews shared a common theme: consistency, reflected in the minor details mentioned repeatedly.
>
> I went on my first morning, right at opening. I sat at the bar and struck up a conversation with Dale, the owner. He asked why I was in town. When I shared that I was

working with a team to improve their customer experience, his face lit up.

"I'm all about the customer experience," he said.

That opened the door to a deeper conversation. He talked about the quality of food. About sourcing from local farms and bakers. When it comes to standards, he and his wife refuse to compromise, even when it would be cheaper or easier.

As we talked, I noticed the other details. An employee was touching up paint where a chair had dinged the rail—the calm pace of the room. The care applied to moments that most customers would never notice. It all seemed routine, and while the breakfast was outstanding, the experience felt deliberate.

I went back the next morning. And the next one. I was curious to watch and learn as they put purpose into practice. Over the week, Dale and I kept circling the same conversation.

- How difficult it is to maintain cultural consistency as something grows.

- How hard it is to scale an owner's mindset.

- How standards have to reach the edges, not stay guarded at the center.

He was clear about one thing: the standard is the standard. Not when it is convenient. Not when leadership is present. Always. For Dale, these weren't posters stating values or reminder memos about culture.

> They were deliberate choices in how work was designed, delivered, and reinforced. The restaurant ran the same way whether or not Dale was there. Expectations were clear and non-negotiable. Dale and his team could name it when they saw it. Their consistency came from structure, not intensity. That is intentionality.

Consistency Beats Intensity

Many leaders believe culture holds in moments of emphasis. A kickoff celebration. Town hall sessions. A video from the CEO. Those moments matter, but they do not endure. Intensity fades while consistency compounds. People build trust through reliable experience.

When behavior holds steady, beliefs follow. This is where organizations struggle most. As teams grow, leaders rely too heavily on existing momentum to maintain standards. They repeat the message. They intervene personally. They correct drift in real time. That approach does not scale. What scales is the design. Clear expectations. Reinforcement embedded in daily work. Standards that do not change based on who is watching or how busy things get. The Half Day Cafe did not feel consistent because everyone seemed to care more. It felt consistent because the structure supported caring.

Consistency reduced effort. It did not demand more of it. This is the shift intentionality requires.

From presence to patterns.

From reminders to reinforcement.

From intensity to durability.

· · ·

When leaders make that shift, identity stops fluctuating. People stop guessing which version of the organization will show up. They know what to expect because they experience it every day. That reliability reinforces values more powerfully than any message ever could.

Intentionality Creates Memory That Outlasts Messaging

Repetition creates memory. Over time, people internalize patterns in how work actually moves. They experience how often plans stay intact versus get reshuffled. Observe whether the work progresses steadily or restarts after an interruption. They see how predictable expectations are across cycles and whether effort builds or dissipates. That memory does not reset when leaders change tone.

After inconsistency, leaders often try to reset direction by stating it more clearly and loudly. To the people doing the work, it feels like something that could change again. People who learned to hedge keep hedging. People who learned to wait keep waiting. People who have learned to stay cautious do not suddenly take risks. They pause and watch to see if the work actually changes.

Behavioral memory reinforces caution more quickly than it reinforces trust. When people adapt to inconsistency, that adaptation becomes efficient and durable. Later attempts to reassert focus rarely land because experience has already taught people how to protect themselves.

Consistency must persist long enough to counter what the system trained them to expect. One aligned decision cannot outweigh ten conflicting ones. A quick burst of follow-through cannot undo months of variability. Intentionality rebuilds as slowly as it eroded.

Leaders who understand this stop asking why people hesitate and start examining what the work has trained them to expect. They focus less on reassurance and more on reliability. Credibility grows through repetition. People respond when the pattern truly changes. Not all at once, but steadily. Judgment returns over time. Initiative expands. Ownership follows because the environment became trustworthy again.

Intentionality Is a Leadership Discipline

Intentionality lasts when it is built into how work actually operates. Leaders often associate intentionality with being visible, sounding committed, and following through personally. Those things matter, but they do not carry over in the long term. What sustains intentionality is consistent discipline. The same priorities get reinforced. The same standards hold under pressure. The same behaviors receive the same response. When those patterns repeat, the work carries the intent. Leadership intervention is no longer necessary to guarantee its success.

When expectations are met, leaders correct less drift and spend more time guiding direction. When reinforcement remains consistent, people stop testing boundaries and start trusting them. Over time, intentionality simplifies leadership. It narrows variables and reduces interpretation cost.

That reliability gives people confidence. They decide with greater certainty. Apply judgment without waiting for permission. And invest more fully because they understand what the work supports. Clear reinforcement allows employees to operate with discretion within understood boundaries. People adapt, respond, and think because they've built reflexes aligned to expectations.

Over time, this discipline shapes identity. The organization becomes recognizable to itself. Culture no longer feels fragile because it no longer depends on reminders. Intentionality is how priorities turn into identity. And once identity holds, connection can take root.

CHAPTER 6

Connection
Why Belonging Sustains Effort

Why Connection Sustains Effort

People often misunderstand connection. Many leaders treat it as a morale issue, a cultural extra, or a byproduct of proximity. Something that improves when teams spend more time together, or leaders show up more visibly. That framing misses the point.

Connection has little to do with closeness and a lot to do with alignment.

People sustain their effort longer in environments where they feel known, where their contributions make sense, and where their presence matters beyond output. Connection answers a different question from clarity or intentionality. It asks whether people see themselves in the work and whether the work reflects something they can stand behind. This is where effort either deepens or contracts.

- ☑ Clear priorities help people execute.
- ☑ Consistent reinforcement helps them trust the system.
- ☐ Connection determines whether people bring judgment, care, and discretionary energy to the work over time.[5]

When connection weakens, people rarely disengage outright. They keep doing their jobs. They meet expectations. They stay professional. What changes is what they no longer offer. Initiative narrows. Risk tolerance drops. Feedback stays safe. Ownership retreats to the boundaries of the role. From the outside, performance can still look strong, which is why disconnection often catches leaders by surprise.

People who feel unseen often continue to deliver. They simply stop offering the additional investment that turns steady performance into resilient performance. Connection changes that dynamic.

When people feel recognized as contributors rather than resources, they engage differently. They speak up sooner. Absorb setbacks with less friction. Stay present during uncertainty because they believe their presence matters. People invest more deeply in environments where they think they belong.

Connection bridges structure and commitment. It allows clarity to carry meaning and intentionality to build trust. Without it, even well-designed systems struggle to elicit discretionary effort.

The Questions People Ask to Decide If They Belong

Connection forms through evaluation. People do it quietly and naturally, through a set of questions they return to as work unfolds.

These questions shape how much effort they offer, how much risk they take, and how long they stay invested.

The questions are simple. Their impact is not.

> *What do I get?*
> This is the anchor of expectations. Pay, schedule, benefits, tools, and clarity all live here. When this answer feels unstable, everything else becomes harder to sustain.

> *What can I give?*
> This defines contribution. People want to know whether their skills matter and whether their judgment counts. When contribution feels constrained or underused, connection weakens, even if satisfaction remains intact.

> *Do I belong?*
> This shapes the risk. Belonging determines whether people speak up, challenge assumptions, or share ideas early. Without it, people are cautious.

> *How can we grow?*
> This indicates forward thinking. Growth includes learning, exposure, challenges, and expanded responsibilities. When growth feels stalled or opaque, effort narrows to the present.

These questions surface at different moments.

Early on, people focus on what they get and what they can give. As work settles, belonging becomes decisive. Over time, growth determines whether investment continues. When any answer becomes unclear, connection weakens even if the performance remains strong. This is where leaders often misread what they are seeing.

People can feel satisfied and disconnected. They can meet expectations and still hold back. They can stay busy and withdraw in quieter ways.

That withdrawal looks controlled. Measured. Professional. And it shapes everything that follows.

Why Disconnection Is Easy to Miss

Disconnection rarely looks like what many leaders imagine disengagement to be. People keep performing. Deadlines hold. Meetings stay civil. Communication remains responsive. From the outside, the work appears steady. What changes is how people participate. In my research with several thousand employees, a clear pattern emerged.

Many of those who described themselves as highly disconnected or apathetic were also among the most successful. They were accomplished, articulate, and highly capable. They understood expectations, navigated the system with ease, and delivered reliably. At the same time, they were psychologically absent from anything beyond what was required. No extra judgment. No advocacy. They disappeared quietly while continuing to deliver. Competence conceals withdrawal.

People limit risk. They keep feedback safe. They avoid exposing unfinished thinking. They focus on execution rather than contribution. None of this disrupts results in the short term. In fact, it often improves predictability—fewer surprises surface. Fewer questions get raised. Teams feel easier to manage. That ease is misleading. Disconnection changes the quality of effort, not its presence. Ideas arrive later. Concerns surface after problems grow. Collaboration narrows to what is necessary. Ownership shrinks to what can be defended. Results hold. Capacity erodes. By the time momentum stalls or attrition rises, people have already adjusted how much of themselves they will bring. What remains looks stable. It simply carries far less room for growth, recovery, or change.

When Connection Becomes Shared

Connection deepens when it stops depending on individual leaders and begins to move through the work itself. When contribution is visible, named, and reinforced by peers, connection becomes shared rather than managed. Belonging no longer flows only from the top. It circulates through daily interactions. This is where connection stops being fragile and starts to require sustained effort. I saw this clearly during my time at Hershey Entertainment & Resorts.

When I joined, the organization had a long list of values. While they existed on paper, few people could name them, and even fewer could connect them to daily work. The intention was sincere. The connection was tenuous.

> A group of us came together to address that gap. In their prior state, the values did not help people decide

how to act, how to prioritize, or how to recognize contribution in real time. We identified the need to connect what the organization promised with how work actually operated. We aligned on four values that described observable behavior: Own. Anticipate. Delight. Inspire.

Each one created a direct line between values and action. People no longer had to interpret meaning. They could recognize it when they saw it.

To reinforce that connection, the organization launched the Legacy Check program in 2010. Team members could recognize associates, on the spot, for actions that reflected the values. The recognition was handwritten, specific, and tied to what someone did and why it mattered. Connection stopped flowing from the top only. Recognition moved laterally. Contribution became visible where the work actually happened, not just during performance cycles.

Over time, a pattern formed. People paid closer attention to one another's efforts. They named behavior aligned with shared standards. They reinforced values through daily interactions. The values began circulating through the work.

From 2022 through mid-2024 alone, the organization distributed more than 36,000 Legacy Checks, valued at over $350,000. The scale matters less than the persistence. Participation persisted because people found meaning in recognizing others and in being recognized in return.

That is shared connection. Belonging becomes observable. Contribution becomes social. Values stop living in statements and start living in relationships.

Connection Is a Leadership Practice

Connection forms when leadership attention becomes predictable. Not constant. Not performative. Reliable. People stay invested when they know their perspective will be sought again, their contribution will be noticed again, and their presence will matter beyond the current moment. Connection weakens when attention arrives only during problems, crises, or performance cycles.

Many organizations rely on personality to create connection. Strong managers. Charismatic leaders. Informal bonds. These help in pockets, but they fluctuate. When attention depends on who is present, how busy things are, or whether something has gone wrong, people adapt quickly. They offer less. They share finished thinking instead of emerging judgment. They wait to be asked rather than stepping forward. Sustained connection requires attention that repeats.

Leaders create connection by consistently returning to what they value. The questions they ask every week, not once. The follow-ups they make predictable. The recognition that shows up without prompting.

When people know their opinions are heard, they stop guarding their perspectives. If recognition naturally becomes part of the workday, people will no longer wonder if their contributions are seen. As inquiry continues and experience grows, connection stabilizes rather than spiking and fading.

This predictability simplifies leadership. Issues surface earlier because people trust they will be addressed. Conversations deepen because unfinished thinking feels safe to share. Effort expands because presence no longer feels conditional. People invest judgment and care when they believe attention will not disappear the moment pressure shifts.

Predictable attention also protects energy. In environments where people feel consistently seen, effort recovers faster. Pressure still exists, but it lands differently. People do not brace for invisibility once the moment passes. They stay engaged because the relationship with the work feels ongoing.

This brings the final rhythm into focus. Recovery is not only about rest. It is about whether work allows energy to return rather than constantly drain it. Connection creates the conditions for that to happen. When people trust that attention, recognition, and inquiry will continue, effort becomes sustainable. And that allows work to endure.

CHAPTER 7
Recovery
Redesigning Work That Restores Energy

Why Recovery Is Misunderstood at Work

Most organizations treat recovery as time away from work. Vacation days. Wellness programs. Mental health benefits. Occasional reminders to disconnect. These tools matter, but they exist outside the work itself. That is the problem.

People view recovery as something they do after work, rather than something the work itself should facilitate. Leaders help people recover from work rather than designing work that doesn't require constant recovery. This framing creates a hidden expectation. People absorb sustained pressure during the workday, then restore themselves on their own time. The system drains energy. Individuals are responsible for replenishing it. That approach does not scale.

In environments where recovery lives outside the work, people adapt by pacing themselves defensively. They ration energy. They limit exposure. They decide where to care and where to conserve. Effort continues, but it becomes calculated rather than expansive. People often mislabel recovery problems as resilience gaps. When energy dips, leaders introduce training. Stress management. Coaching on boundaries.

These tools support people without changing their work. They help people cope. They do not address the conditions that create depletion.

Operationally, recovery depends on four elements that leaders control.

> **Pace.**
>
> Work needs moments of intensity and moments of settling. When urgency becomes permanent, people never regain baseline energy. Judgment degrades because everything feels critical.

> **Boundaries.**
>
> Clear starts and stops matter. When work bleeds continuously across time, cognitive load accumulates even when people are technically off.

> **Decision.**
>
> Every unresolved decision consumes energy. Too many unclear choices accelerate fatigue. Simplifying decisions restores energy faster than reducing hours.

> **Stability.**
>
> Work that changes constantly demands constant vigilance. When priorities or standards shift unpredictably, energy shifts toward monitoring rather than execution.

These elements determine whether recovery is present in the work. When these elements are absent, people must borrow recovery time from nights, weekends, and vacations. That debt grows larger over time. Organizations that understand this stop asking people to be more resilient and start making work more recoverable. They design for optimum energy, not extensive endurance.

The Hidden Cost of Always-On Work
Always-on work often looks like responsiveness. Messages get answered quickly. Decisions happen in real time. Teams stay available. But when urgency becomes the default, recovery disappears from the system.

There is no settling point. No return to baseline. People remain partially activated even when nothing is actively urgent.[6] That constant activation drains energy—attention fragments. Thinking becomes reactive. Work shifts from methodical to continuous triage.

Operationally, work stops finishing. Tasks move forward without closure. Decisions remain provisional. Conversations restart instead of resolving. Progress looks busy but rarely feels complete. The incomplete work creates a backlog. Open loops compete for attention. Mental effort accumulates even when work pauses.

Leaders often mistake this for efficiency. Speed looks like momentum. Availability looks like commitment. What they are really seeing is compensation. People work longer to avoid falling behind. They respond faster to prevent escalation. They over-commit themselves to keep pace.

These behaviors maintain output while steadily depleting energy. Always-on environments also distort prioritization. When everything feels urgent, sequencing breaks down. People respond to visibility rather than importance. Activity replaces direction. Recovery requires contrast. Periods of intensity must be followed by periods of stabilization. Without that variance, effort flattens into endurance. Over time, teams adapt. The work continues. Capacity does not.

Burnout Is a Lagging Indicator

Burnout shows up after the system has already failed. Not when energy first declines, but after people have compensated for its absence for too long. Operationally, burnout is not an early warning. It is a trailing indicator that sustained effort has been unsupported.

Long before exhaustion becomes visible, the work changes. People absorb instability that should have been resolved structurally. They manage vague priorities manually. They close gaps between misaligned decisions. Output continues because people compensate. Leaders often mistake this for strength. The team keeps delivering. Problems stay contained. Pressure does not escalate upward. But really, it's just energy being redirected.

Instead of investing in improvement, people stabilize the present. Instead of extending judgment, they simplify decisions. Instead of building momentum, they maintain balance. Top performers feel this first.

They become default stabilizers. Complexity flows toward them. Recovery remains unavailable while they work to resolve issues. Burnout arrives later, when that capacity finally runs out. By then, organizations respond at the individual level.

Support appears. The work remains unchanged. It's for this reason that burnout interventions disappoint. Rest addresses depletion. It does not remove the conditions that caused it. When people return, the same workload awaits.

Burnout points to a single failure. The system consumed energy faster than it could replenish it.[7]

Focusing on who burned out misses the problem. The real question is where recovery became impossible during the work itself. Where urgency never settled. Where decisions are never closed. Until leaders confront why work requires people to recover from it, rather than within it, burnout will keep appearing as a personal outcome of a structural design flaw.

What Changes When Recovery Exists

When you build recovery into the work, effort takes on a different shape. People do not work less. They work with greater capacity.

The first shift appears in judgment. Decisions improve because people are no longer operating at the edge of depletion. They weigh trade-offs more accurately. Context replaces reflex.

Next, the pace stabilizes. Work stops swinging between urgency and exhaustion. Completion improves because work settles before the next demand arrives. Escalations decrease—rework declines. Recovery also restores adaptability.

Teams respond calmly to change. They adjust sequencing rather than abandoning direction. Change becomes manageable rather than destabilizing.

Leaders feel the shift, too. They intervene less. They spend less time smoothing friction and more time guiding direction. Progress feels steadier because the system carries more of the load. Recovery strengthens the other rhythms.

* * *

Clarity holds because priorities remain stable.
Intentionality compounds because reinforcement survives pressure.
Connection deepens because people have energy beyond execution.
Recovery allows momentum to persist.

* * *

When energy is restored, the effort in the work is compounded rather than reset to zero. This is the outcome leaders should expect. Capacity. Stability. Work that absorbs pressure without breaking. Recovery does not lower standards. It allows organizations to meet them consistently.

When the Rhythm Holds, Purpose Endures
Clarity sets direction. Intentionality makes it trustworthy. Connection keeps people invested. Recovery allows effort to compound instead of collapse.

When anyone fails, purpose weakens. People guess. Hesitate. Withdraw. Endure. Each failure compounds the others. Purpose weakens when the system cannot sustain the effort required to live it.

Purpose depends on rhythm. It holds when the pace becomes

predictable, when energy can return without stopping everything, when effort feels like an investment rather than a sacrifice.

Organizations designed around endurance ask people to carry the load personally. Organizations designed around rhythm distribute the load through structure. That difference determines whether purpose survives pressure.

When rhythm holds, people stop asking whether the effort is worth it. They feel the answer through daily work. The system reinforces it. The work carries it.

CHAPTER 8

The Leader's Role in Making Purpose Real

Leadership Is a Design Role, Not a Messaging Role

With purpose, most leaders spend far more time shaping words than shaping work. They debate language, refine statements, and workshop phrasing they hope will inspire belief. When belief fades, they return to the same playbook. Clearer language. Stronger framing. More communication. It feels responsible. It also misses the problem.

Purpose weakens when the work people do sends a message that differs from the one leaders promoted. Daily priorities, decision rules, incentives, and trade-offs teach people what actually matters. That teaching happens continuously, whether leaders intend it or not. Purpose becomes real through structure. Through how work functions under pressure, not how it is described.

Every decision creates a constraint.

Every constraint teaches behavior.

Every reinforcement trains people how to succeed inside the system as it actually exists.

Over time, these patterns outweigh intent. Leaders make purpose real by deciding what the work requires people to do repeatedly to succeed. That is the leadership role most organizations overlook.

The question stops being, *"Do you believe in the purpose?"* The question becomes, *"What does your system require people to do to survive here?"*

Every leader already runs an operating system. Some are deliberate. Many are accidental. All of them teach people how to behave.

The accurate measure of leadership is not how people behave when leaders are watching. It is how work behaves when they are not. If purpose depends on constant explanation, escalation, and reinforcement from the top, the system is unfinished. This chapter resets the leadership job.

Leadership is Pattern Ownership

Leadership succeeds through patterns that hold. Every organization runs on repeatable behaviors. The system makes them unavoidable. Over time, intentionally designed or not, those patterns become the real operating rules of the business. This is where leadership responsibility lives.

Leaders do not own every decision. They own the patterns those decisions create. What repeats without permission. What holds without escalation. What people trust to remain true when conditions change. When leaders intervene constantly, they teach dependence. When leaders design patterns that reinforce themselves, they teach judgment. Strong leadership reduces the need for presence. It replaces correction with constraint. It shifts responsibility from individual performance to system behavior. The goal is alignment through predictability. If work behaves differently depending on who is in the room, leadership has not done its job.

The sections that follow define the six non-delegable pattern decisions leaders must own. Each one corresponds to a core element of the RHYTHM Operating System.

Together, they determine whether purpose survives pressure or collapses into improvisation.

R — Resolve What Matters (Clarity)

Clarity is achieved by resolving the conflicts among priorities. Most leadership teams believe they have clarity because they can list their priorities. The real test is whether those priorities survive contact with trade-offs. If everything remains important, nothing is resolved.

Your job is not to explain focus. Your job is to eliminate ambiguity that the organization cannot eliminate on its own. That work starts with resolution, not alignment.

The First Leadership Question: What Breaks First?
If demand increases by 20 percent next quarter, what gives? If you cannot answer that question immediately, the system lacks clarity.

Leaders must explicitly decide:
- Which priorities outrank others when capacity is constrained?
- Which commitments will pause, slow, or stop when pressure rises?
- Which work will disappoint someone by design?

Until those decisions are made, teams are forced to guess. Guessing creates delay, escalation, and defensive execution.

Make Trade-offs Visible, Not Implied

Clarity collapses when trade-offs stay implicit. You cannot expect teams to sequence work correctly if leadership only communicates intent and not displacement. Every priority decision must include a companion decision: what this displaces.

In practice, this means leaders must get comfortable answering questions like:

- "If we say yes to this, what are we saying no to?"
- "What stops moving when this starts?"
- "What work becomes less important because this exists?"

If those answers live only in executive conversations, clarity will not scale.

Fix the Meeting Where Clarity Actually Breaks

Clarity rarely fails in strategy decks. It fails in recurring forums. Look at the meetings where work gets assigned, escalated, or re-scoped. Those are the moments where leaders either resolve ambiguity or pass it downstream.

In those moments, leaders must:

- Force prioritization before assigning work.
- Reject vague urgency.
- Refuse to accept commitments that exceed capacity without renegotiation.

If leaders allow ambiguity in those forums, no amount of clarity elsewhere will hold.

> In a SaaS company, leaders repeatedly approved sales-driven sprint work without stopping any other work. Core product work slid quietly, sprint after sprint.
>
> During interviews, engineers described the same moment every cycle. "We didn't know which promise would get us in trouble for missing," one said. "So we made our best guess and punted what we could." Work slowed as teams buffered risk rather than committing fully.
>
> Deadlines blurred. Fixes waited. Customer escalations rose after issues were traced back to postponed core work.
>
> The pattern finally broke during a leadership review that paused a sales sprint before approving another. One engineer captured the shift: "That was the first time it felt like someone had our back."
>
> Inside the company, that meeting became known as the sprint where guessing stopped.

Questions Leaders Should Be Asking Relentlessly

To operationalize clarity, leaders should regularly ask:
- "What are we asking people to hold at the same time that may be incompatible?"
- "Where have we failed to remove work when adding new demand?"
- "Which priorities are we protecting with words but undermining with decisions?"
- "Where are teams escalating because we have not resolved trade-offs?"

These questions are uncomfortable by design. They surface the decisions leaders have been avoiding.

H — Hold the Line (Intentionality)

Intentionality is about consistency under pressure, not principles. Most leadership teams believe they are intentional because they have principles, standards, and stated priorities. The real test is whether those principles survive inconvenience. When trade-offs become uncomfortable, many leaders quietly bend rather than hold. People notice immediately.

Intentionality is not what leaders intend to reinforce. It is what the system reinforces when exceptions appear. Every response teaches people how seriously to take what was said before. Your job is not to defend values rhetorically. Your job is to make reinforcement predictable.

The First Leadership Question: What Will We Still Enforce When It Hurts?

- When a deadline slips, what matters more? Speed or quality?
- When performance is strong, but behavior is misaligned, what gets reinforced?
- When a high performer violates a standard, what happens next?

If the answers depend on circumstance, mood, or who is involved, intentionality does not exist. The system is teaching people to test boundaries rather than to trust them.

Leaders must explicitly decide:
- Which standards will hold even when outcomes are at risk?
- Which behaviors earn reinforcement consistently?
- Which exceptions exist, and why they exist.

Until those decisions are explicit, reinforcement will waft under pressure.

Stop Making Exceptions Quietly

Intentionality fractures fastest through silent exceptions. Leaders twist rules to keep things moving. They override decisions to avoid conflict. They tolerate misalignment because "this one time" feels justified. Each time, the system learns that standards are negotiable. If an exception is necessary, it must be named.

In practice, this means leaders must be willing to say:
- "We are breaking our usual rule, and here is why."
- "This does not set a precedent."
- "Here is what still holds, even though this outcome changed."

Silence erodes trust faster than disagreement.

Reinforcement Must Be Boring to Be Believable

Intentionality strengthens when reinforcement becomes predictable. Leaders often confuse intensity with impact. They overcorrect. They intervene dramatically. They send assertive signs inconsistently. This trains vigilance, not confidence.

Instead, leaders must:
- Respond to the same behaviors the same way over time.
- Reinforce standards even when it slows progress.
- Allow consequences to play out instead of rescuing outcomes.

When reinforcement becomes boring, people stop testing it.

Where Intentionality Actually Breaks

Intentionality rarely breaks in value statements. It breaks in moments of inconvenience.

Look at:

- Performance reviews where results excuse behavior.
- Escalations where leaders override agreed-upon rules.
- Crisis moments where standards quietly disappear.

Those are the moments that define the system. If leaders want intentionality to hold, they must protect standards in precisely those situations.

> At a manufacturing organization, leaders maintained a clear set of operating standards. Overtime required explicit approval and documentation so leaders could see where work was straining and respond deliberately.
>
> During a peak-demand period, overtime approvals increased, as expected. What surprised leaders came afterward. As volume normalized, overtime kept getting approved with less scrutiny. It stopped prompting questions and started smoothing schedules.
>
> Supervisors described the shift, *"it eventually felt like something we didn't really need to call out."*
>
> Overtime reduced short-term friction. It made planning easier. What went unnoticed was what it obscured. Labor costs rose unevenly. Fatigue concentrated in a few teams.
>
> Leaders lost a clear view of where the work actually needed attention. Instead of revealing stress points, overtime blended them into the background.

The pattern changed during a routine review when a leader reinstated the expectation. Overtime was still allowed. What changed was that it had to surface again.

"If it's happening," he said, "we need to see it."

After that, overtime approvals stabilized. Supervisors planned with clearer constraints. Leaders regained sightlines into where the work required redesign instead of quiet accommodation. Intentionality returned when the standard stopped fading into habit and started shaping behavior again.

Questions Leaders Should Be Asking Relentlessly

To operationalize intentionality, leaders should regularly ask:
- "Where have we rewarded outcomes that violated our standards?"
- "Which exceptions have we made without explanation?"
- "What behaviors are people testing repeatedly?"
- "Where are leaders stepping in instead of letting reinforcement do its job?"

These questions surface the gap between stated values and lived reinforcement.

Y — You Belong Here (Connection)

Connection is not created through culture statements or team-building exercises. It forms when people can see how their effort matters and know it will be recognized without personal sacrifice. Most leaders believe connection comes from more visibly caring. In practice, it comes from designing work so that the contribution is unmistakable.

When people cannot see how their work fits in, they disconnect to conserve energy. Your job is not to manufacture belonging. Your job is to remove the conditions that make people feel interchangeable.

The First Leadership Question: What Counts Here?

In every organization, people are already answering this question for themselves.

- What kind of effort gets noticed?
- What kind of work gets rewarded?
- What kind of behavior advances your standing?

If the answers point to endurance, availability, or personal sacrifice, connection will degrade no matter how inclusive the language sounds.

Leaders must explicitly decide:
- What does a meaningful contribution look like in this system?
- What outcomes matter more than optics?
- What behaviors signal value without requiring heroics?

Until those decisions are clear, people will default to what feels safest.

Stop Confusing Sacrifice With Commitment

Connection erodes fastest when sacrifice becomes the signal of value. Late nights get praised. Rapid responses get noticed. Personal boundaries get quietly penalized. Over time, people learn that belonging requires depletion. That lesson never produces engagement. It produces withdrawal.

Leaders must stop:
- Praising effort that compensates for broken systems.
- Equating availability with commitment.
- Treating burnout as evidence of dedication.

If people have to give more of themselves to be seen, connection will not hold.

Make Contribution Visible in the Flow of Work

Connection strengthens when contribution is observable without narration.

Leaders create this by:
- Naming impact accurately and specifically.
- Tying recognition to shared standards, not personal strain.
- Highlighting how individual work advances collective outcomes.

Recognition should clarify what matters, not spotlight who tolerated the most. If leaders must constantly explain why someone's work mattered, the system is not doing enough of that work itself.

Where Connection Actually Breaks
Connection does not break because people lack purpose. It breaks when effort disappears into the system without acknowledgment or consequence.

Look at:
- Work that is essential but invisible.
- Roles where success is defined by the absence of failure.
- Teams that deliver reliably but receive attention only when something breaks.

Those are the fault lines where disengagement forms. Leaders do not fix this with appreciation campaigns. They fix it by redesigning how contributions show up.

> I worked in a department that merged with several others after a major organizational change. Leaders lost roles. Teams were reshuffled. People were placed under new managers who didn't know their history. Some didn't even know if they still had a future there.

The mood was heavy. People held information closely. Conversations stayed surface-level. Every interaction carried an unspoken question: Am I safe here, or am I next? You could feel people trying to prove their value. Staying visible. Saying yes quickly. Making sure their effort didn't go unnoticed.

Rather than letting that dynamic harden, we (the leaders) slowed things down. Managers started scheduling one-on-ones with people they didn't already know. Not to motivate or reassure them, but to understand what they actually worked on and where they were getting stuck. Coffee meetings followed, often awkward at first. People were cautious about what they shared.

Over time, something shifted.

People realized they didn't have to perform to be seen. Their work was already visible once someone took the time to understand it. Quiet contributions began to be referenced in meetings. Dependencies were acknowledged. Effort showed up without being dramatic.

The fear didn't disappear overnight. But the tone changed. People stopped posturing as much. They shared context sooner. They asked for help without feeling exposed. Connection didn't form because we asked people to trust us. It formed because the work stopped making people feel interchangeable.

Belonging became possible once contribution could be recognized without asking people to give more of themselves to earn it. Connection happened because

> the system answered a simple question through action:
> *This is how your contribution matters here.*

Questions Leaders Should Be Asking Relentlessly

To operationalize connection, leaders should regularly ask:
- "Which contributions are essential but unseen?"
- "Who is carrying the load without recognition?"
- "Where have we confused endurance with impact?"
- "What work would go unnoticed if someone stopped doing it?"

These questions arise as to whether belonging is built into the system or dependent on visibility and proximity.

T — Tempo the Work (Recovery)

Recovery is determined by how work is paced, not by how resilient people are. Most leaders believe recovery is a personal responsibility. Time off, boundaries, and self-management get framed as individual choices.

In reality, recovery emerges from how demand enters the system, how long it remains active, and whether work is allowed to complete before more arrives. Your job is not to encourage people to recharge. Your job is to prevent the system from requiring constant activation.

The First Leadership Question: What Is the Default Pace?

Every organization has a tempo, whether it has been chosen or not.

- Is urgency occasional or constant?
- Does work arrive in waves or as an uninterrupted stream?
- Do priorities settle or stack?

If pressure never releases, recovery never occurs. People respond by conserving energy, narrowing judgment, and doing only what is required to endure.

Leaders must explicitly decide:

- At what pace can the system sustain without depleting?
- Where work must slow, pause, or finish.
- Which demands require intensity and which do not?

Without these decisions, urgency becomes ambient, and exhaustion becomes structural.

Stop Treating Urgency as a Virtue

Tempo breaks when urgency turns into posture. Short-term pressure has a purpose. Long-term pressure erodes performance. When everything is framed as critical, people lose the ability to distinguish true priorities.

Leaders must stop:
- Signaling importance through speed alone.
- Adding demand without removing load.
- Allowing deadlines to compress indefinitely.

Urgency should be used intentionally, not habitually.

Design for Completion, Not Perpetual Motion

Recovery depends on completion. Work that never fully finishes keeps people cognitively engaged even when tasks change. Open loops drain energy faster than long hours.

Leaders create recovery by:
- Defining what "done" actually means.
- Allowing work to settle before introducing new demand.
- Resisting the urge to stack initiatives without closure.

When completion disappears, people never give up. Performance degrades even as activity increases.

Protect Energy Through Structural Boundaries

Boundaries that rely on personal discipline will fail under pressure. Boundaries that are structural will hold.

Leaders must be willing to:
- Limit decision load during peak periods.
- Protect non-negotiable recovery windows.
- Interrupt patterns that require constant availability.

If boundaries collapse the moment pressure rises, they were never real to begin with.

> I worked with a contact center that received a clear mandate from the executive team. Contact volume was increasing. Staffing would remain flat. Service level had to hold.
>
> Leaders were encouraged to manage the gap creatively. Push customers toward self-service. Reduce avoidable contacts. Tighten processes. The math was unforgiving, but the expectation was firm.
>
> Over time, the impact showed up in one place. Agent occupancy rose steadily. The small gaps between contacts disappeared. Calls still varied in complexity, but one interaction now flowed directly into the next with no pause. On the floor, people felt the change immediately.
>
> Even routine calls required more effort. There was no time to reset before the next customer arrived. Agents described feeling "on" from the first interaction of the day to the last, regardless of what the call required.

Supervisors began noticing subtle shifts. Agents relied more heavily on scripts. Judgment narrowed late in shifts. The same people who were usually steady started having uneven days. Not because they cared less, but because the pace left no room to recover attention.

Leadership initially responded by pressing the same levers harder. More emphasis on deflection. More scrutiny of efficiency. Each move protected service level, but further compressed the day.

What finally forced a reset wasn't burnout or attrition. It was variability. Quality became less predictable. Coaching conversations shifted from development to containment. The system was no longer stable.

At that point, leaders revisited the original constraint. Volume was up. Staffing was flat. Service level mattered. Something still had to give. They chose pace.

Occupancy targets were reset to restore brief recovery windows between contacts. Not long breaks. Just enough space for one interaction to finish before the next began. Certain call types were deliberately throttled during peak hours. Noncritical demand was deferred instead of stacked.

Service level dipped slightly in the short term. Quality stabilized quickly. Within weeks, late-shift errors declined and coaching returned to growth rather than correction.

Nothing about the people changed. Nothing about the

> work changed. The tempo did.
>
> Recovery returned once the system stopped demanding uninterrupted attentiveness and allowed people to complete one interaction before starting the next.

Questions Leaders Should Be Asking Relentlessly

To operationalize tempo, leaders should regularly ask:
- "Where have we normalized sustained urgency?"
- "What work never truly completes?"
- "Where are people staying activated longer than necessary?"
- "What demand could wait but is being pulled forward?"

These questions reveal whether the system renews energy or consumes it.

H — Hear the System (Measurement)

Every system is already communicating. The question is whether leaders are paying attention to the right evidence. Most organizations collect enormous amounts of data. Very little of it reflects how work is actually experienced. Performance metrics dominate. Lived experience gets discounted. Early indicators of strain surface late, after energy and trust have already eroded.

Hearing the system requires leaders to tune into friction, strain, and distortion while those conditions are still reversible. Your job is not to measure more. Your job is to listen earlier and respond deliberately.

The First Leadership Question: What Is the System Revealing Before Results Slip?

By the time performance declines, the information is already stale. Work communicates stress long before it breaks. Through rework. Through hesitation. Through escalation patterns. Through the quiet emergence of workarounds.

Leaders must explicitly decide:
- Which patterns indicate rising friction?
- Which behaviors suggest people are compensating rather than executing?
- Which conditions show effort increasing without corresponding clarity or impact?

If leaders wait for lagging results, they are managing consequences, not systems.

Stop Treating Experience Data as Secondary

Measurement breaks down when leaders separate experience from performance. They trust output metrics and discount lived experience as subjective. In doing so, they lose access to the earliest evidence of system health.

Leaders must stop:

- Treating employee feedback as anecdotal.
- Dismissing recurring friction because it lacks numerical precision.
- Waiting for failure to legitimize discomfort.

Experience data does not compete with performance data. It explains it.

Decide What You Will Pay Attention To

Hearing the system requires intent.

Leaders must decide in advance:

- Which indicators warrant attention?
- Where those indicators will be reviewed.
- What types of responses do different conditions require?

Without these decisions, information surfaces inconsistently, and action becomes unpredictable. Listening is a design choice, not a personality trait.

Fix the Moment Where Information Goes Quiet

Most systems do not fail loudly. They fail quietly.

Information disappears when:

- People stop raising friction because nothing changes.
- Escalation feels risky.
- Feedback loops close without acknowledgment.

Leaders must protect the pathways where work communicates strain. When input does not reliably lead to a response, people conserve energy by staying silent.

Questions Leaders Should Be Asking Relentlessly

To operationalize system listening, leaders should regularly ask:
- "Where is work getting harder without a clear cause?"
- "What workarounds have become normal?"
- "Where are people compensating instead of escalating?"
- "What patterns keep recurring without resolution?"

These questions surface strain while they can still be addressed.

M — Make It Repeat (Cadence)

Cadence is how leadership intent survives time, turnover, and distraction. It is the repeatable rhythm through which priorities are revisited, standards are reinforced, and course corrections are made without requiring urgency or presence. Cadence is not a meeting schedule. It is the mechanism that allows judgment to scale.

Most leadership teams underestimate cadence because they confuse it with control. They worry that repetition will create rigidity. In practice, the opposite happens. Without cadence, leaders are forced to intervene constantly. With cadence, the system self-corrects.

Cadence answers a simple question that most organizations leave unresolved:

When and how does the system reinforce what matters?

If the answer is "when someone notices" or "when something goes wrong," cadence does not exist.

How Cadence Actually Works

Cadence creates expectation before instruction.

People know:
- When will priorities be reviewed?
- When trade-offs will be addressed.
- When will standards be reinforced?
- When pressure will be reassessed.

Because those moments are predictable, people stop waiting for permission. Judgment improves because reinforcement is no longer arbitrary. Cadence replaces vigilance with confidence. Leaders do not need to remind people what matters when the system reliably returns to it.

The First Leadership Question: Where Does Reinforcement Live?

In most organizations, reinforcement fluctuates. Sometimes it happens in meetings. Sometimes in one-on-ones. Sometimes in crisis. Sometimes not at all. The inconsistency forces people to read personalities instead of patterns.

Leaders must decide:
- Where priorities are revisited, regardless of conditions.
- Where trade-offs are renegotiated, not improvised.
- Where standards are reinforced even when nothing is broken.

Until reinforcement has a home, cadence cannot form.

Cadence Is the Difference Between Memory and Design

Without cadence, leaders rely on memory. They remember to check in. They remember to reinforce. They remember to correct. When attention shifts, reinforcement disappears. The system drifts. With cadence, memory becomes irrelevant. Reinforcement happens because the rhythm demands it, not because a leader remembered to do it. That is the difference between leadership effort and organizational reliability.

Questions Leaders Should Be Asking Relentlessly

To operationalize cadence, leaders should regularly ask:
- "Where do we only reinforce priorities when something breaks?"
- "What expectations depend on who is in the room?"
- "Where are people waiting for permission because reinforcement is unpredictable?"
- "Which decisions get revisited consistently, and which only resurface during conflict?"
- "If I stepped away for thirty days, what patterns would hold and which would drift?"

These questions expose where cadence exists and where leadership presence is still doing the work of design.

From Design to Evidence

Design decisions only matter if they change how work is experienced.

Leaders can resolve priorities, hold standards, make contributions visible, pace demand, listen for strain, and reinforce through cadence. None of it holds if leaders rely on assumptions instead of evidence.

Most breakdowns do not announce themselves. They accumulate. Small accommodations become normal. Workarounds replace judgment. Effort increases to compensate for design gaps. By the time results reflect the cost, people have already adapted in ways leaders never intended. This is where leadership accountability sharpens.

If you are serious about making purpose real, you must be willing to examine how work actually feels, not how you believe it operates. You must replace intuition with visibility. You must stop relying on lagging outcomes to explain conditions people have already learned to endure.

The next chapter focuses on that work. Not measurement as reporting. Not metrics as justification. But measurement as a way of understanding what the system is producing before damage becomes visible.

Purpose does not vanish in a moment. It degrades while leaders remain confident that things are fine. Chapter 9 is about learning to recognize degradation early and respond before people are forced to give less of themselves than the work truly requires.

CHAPTER 9
Measuring What Work Actually Feels Like

Why Leaders Measure the Wrong Things

Most leaders believe they already measure what matters. They track performance. They review outcomes. They monitor productivity, quality, speed, and cost. When results hold, they assume the system is healthy. When results slip, they go looking for causes. The problem lies in timing.

Outcomes lag experience. By the time performance changes, people have already been adapting, compensating, or conserving effort for quite a while. Leaders manage effects while remaining blind to causes. This creates a dangerous illusion.

As long as the results look stable, leaders assume the work experience is fine. They treat strain as temporary, effort as sustainable, and pressure as manageable. In reality, people often protect performance by absorbing instability personally. They carry confusion. They bridge gaps. They compensate for poor process and unclear decisions.

The system appears strong. The cost stays hidden. This is why leaders feel blindsided when momentum stalls or attrition spikes. The warning patterns existed. Traditional metrics never surfaced the problem because leaders measure what they can quantify easily.

Revenue. Throughput. Utilization. Defects. These measures matter.

They describe what the system produces. They fail to describe what the system demands from people to produce it.

Understanding that distinction is vital for leaders.

Two teams can deliver identical results while operating under radically different levels of effort, strain, and risk. One team works inside a system that supports judgment and recovery. The other survives through constant compensation. Standard metrics treat them as equivalent. The work experience does not.

When leaders rely exclusively on outcomes, they miss early evidence that work has grown heavier, noisier, or more fragile. They discover problems only after people adjust to protect themselves. At that point, measurement turns reactive.

This is why leaders reach for surveys when something feels off. They sense a gap between results and energy and look for a way to quantify sentiment. Surveys promise insight without disrupting operations. They arrive late. By the time people articulate frustration, the system has already shaped behavior.

Surveys capture reflection after adaptation, not the conditions that produced it. The last thing leaders need is more opinion data to understand what work feels like. They need to learn how to read the work itself.

Work reveals its experience through behavior. Through how decisions move. Through how often issues escalate. Through how much effort goes into coordination versus creation. Through how people pace themselves under pressure. Leaders see this evidence every day.

Most never treat it as a measurement.

This chapter centers measurement on effort, friction, and strain as operational realities. Because what work feels like does not live in sentiment. It lives in design. And design leaves evidence.

From Outcomes to Evidence

Leaders already have access to what they need to understand how work feels. What's missing is a disciplined way of reading what the work is already showing. The purpose of measurement here is early visibility. Leaders need to see strain while performance still holds, while people quietly compensate, and while minor design adjustments can prevent larger failures. That requires paying attention to how work moves, not just what it produces.

We're going to focus on three observable patterns that surface during normal operations. They appear before results change and before people articulate frustration. They require no surveys, no new dashboards, and no additional reporting cycles. They show up in the meetings leaders attend, the work they review, and the decisions they touch every week.

> Each pattern answers a specific question about the system:
> - How easily do decisions move?
> - Does work reach clear completion?
> - Where does the effort pool instead of spreading?

Together, these patterns offer a practical way to understand how experience forms. They reflect effort, friction, and strain as operational realities, not opinions. Leaders already encounter this evidence daily. The shift is learning to treat it as a measurement rather than background noise. Instead of asking people to interpret their experience, leaders observe how the system behaves under normal conditions. Instead of waiting for results to change, leaders notice when work slows, stacks up, or relies on compensation to hold.

Each section that follows takes a single pattern and does three things:
1. Identifies how it shows up in everyday work.
2. Points to where leaders can observe it immediately using existing tools and forums.
3. Describes the most minor structural adjustment that interrupts the pattern.

When leaders read these patterns consistently, measurement becomes directional. It informs where to act first and what kind of change will matter. The work itself provides the evidence. The first pattern becomes visible wherever decisions are hesitated.

Decision Friction: When Judgment Becomes Risky
Decision friction forms when people stop trusting that a decision will hold.

It often shows up as caution. Extra alignment. Repeated confirmation. Escalation framed as diligence. On the surface, the organization appears thoughtful and disciplined. Beneath it, judgment constricts.

People hesitate when they cannot predict what will happen after a decision. They slow down because priorities shift without warning. They escalate because past decisions were quietly overridden. They revisit agreements because exceptions appeared later without explanation.

Over time, the system teaches a clear lesson: waiting is safer than acting. That lesson reshapes how work moves long before performance changes.

Where Decision Friction Shows Up First

Decision friction is visible in the flow of work, not in sentiment or outcomes. Leaders see it every week, often without naming it.

Pay attention to:

Decision velocity
- How long does it take for a decision to turn into action?
- Where does work pause after agreement?
- Which decisions remain reversible far longer than expected?

Decision elevation
- Which decisions escalate that previously did not?
- Where does ownership blur at the moment of commitment?
- How often do people seek validation instead of acting?

Decision recycling
- Which topics resurface repeatedly without resolution?
- Where does "alignment" replace execution?
- Which decisions never quite close?

These patterns show up clearly in:

- Standing agendas with recurring unresolved items.
- Task systems where work stalls after "decision made."
- Email threads that grow after agreement instead of shrinking.
- Calendars filled with follow-up meetings instead of execution time.

Ask yourself: *After a decision is made, does the work move or hesitate?*

What to Pay Attention to Without Adding Overhead

Decision friction can be tracked through simple observation, using artifacts that leaders already review.

Examples leaders can examine weekly:

- How many decisions were reopened after initial agreement?
- The time between the decision and the first visible action.
- Escalation frequency for similar decision types.
- Meeting time spent revisiting past decisions.

These indicators do not need formal targets or dashboards. When these patterns intensify, decision friction rises.

The Smallest Structural Shift That Restores Confidence

When leaders notice decision friction, the instinct is to explain more. That instinct often reinforces hesitation. What changes behavior fastest is reducing uncertainty about what will hold.

A practical intervention sequence:

Classify the decision
- Is it reversible or irreversible?
- Who owns it, and who provides input?

State the durability
- How long is this decision expected to stand?
- What conditions justify revisiting it?

Clarify escalation limits
- When escalation applies.
- When it does not.

Allow the decision to stand
- Resist revisiting it prematurely.
- Let the system experience stability.

One decision that holds consistently reshapes behavior faster than repeated reassurance.

Why This Changes the Feel of Work Quickly

Decision friction taxes the organization quietly. It pulls leaders into unnecessary escalation. It delays execution without appearing idle. It shifts effort from judgment to protection. When leaders address friction structurally, work accelerates without urgency. People act sooner because they trust the system to support their decisions. Confidence returns before morale does.

In complex operating environments, rising decision friction is often the earliest visible sign that the system no longer reliably reinforces purpose. Leaders who address it directly often stabilize execution without changing goals, teams, or incentives. This is why decision friction is the first place to look when measuring what work actually feels like.

What Becomes Visible Next
Once decisions begin to hold, another pattern emerges. Work either reaches a clear end state or continues to accumulate without closure. That pattern determines whether energy is returned or drained. This is where the integrity of completion becomes visible.

Completion Integrity: When Work Never Fully Lands
Completion integrity determines whether work is allowed to finish before new demand arrives. When completion holds, effort releases. Attention resets—energy returns inside execution. When completion breaks, work lingers. People move on physically while remaining cognitively engaged. Open loops accumulate. Recovery disappears from the work itself.

Leaders often miss this pattern because activity stays high. Output continues. Meetings stay full. The system looks productive. The cost shows up quietly as fatigue, irritability, and reduced judgment long before performance changes. Completion integrity reveals whether the system creates closure or perpetual motion.

Where Incompletion Becomes Normal

Leaders see incomplete work constantly. It often hides in plain sight.

Pay attention to:

Work carryover

- Tasks that roll forward unchanged across cycles.
- Initiatives that remain "almost done" for weeks or months.
- Priorities that reset before earlier commitments close.

Context drag

- Work that requires repeated re-explanation.
- Decisions are revisited because context is never settled.
- Teams that spend more time re-orienting than advancing.

Deferred closure

- Outcomes are defined vaguely to preserve flexibility.
- Success is measured by activity rather than completion.
- Work that stays active because stopping feels risky.

These patterns show up clearly in:

- Status reports that repeat without progress.
- Backlogs that churn instead of shrinking.
- Calendars filled with follow-ups rather than finishes.
- Projects that blur into the next initiative without closure.

Ask yourself: *Does work actually finish, or does it just move?*

What to Pay Attention to Without Adding Overhead

Completion integrity can be observed by examining:

- Percentage of work that closes versus carries forward.
- Number of initiatives active beyond their original window.
- Frequency of priority resets before completion.
- Time between "nearly done" and actual closure.

When completion erodes, energy drains inside execution. The work feels heavier even when output remains high.

The Smallest Structural Shift That Restores Closure

When completion breaks down, leaders often increase urgency. They push for faster delivery. They tighten deadlines. Activity increases. Closure does not. What restores completion is protecting the finish.

A practical intervention sequence:

> **Define what done means**
> - What condition indicates completion?
> - What does not need to happen for work to end?

> **Protect the close**
> - Do not introduce new demand into unfinished work.
> - Avoid layering "just one more thing" onto active commitments.

Create space for settling
- Allow work to land before redirecting effort.
- Let ownership release before reassignment.

Let one cycle finish cleanly
- Resist interrupting the close.
- Allow the system to experience completion.

One visible finish teaches the organization that closure matters more than constant motion.

Why This Changes the Feel of Work Quickly

Incomplete work creates a background workload. It consumes attention even when people move on. It compresses recovery inside execution. It encourages defensive pacing. When work finishes cleanly, cognitive load drops. Energy returns without requiring time off. Judgment improves because attention is no longer split across unresolved commitments.

In operational redesign and transformation work, persistent fatigue is rarely driven solely by volume. It is driven by unfinished work stacking invisibly over time. Leaders who restore completion integrity often see energy rebound without changing headcount, tooling, or goals.

What Becomes Visible Next

When work is allowed to finish, a third pattern surfaces. Effort either distributes naturally or pools around specific people and roles. That pattern reveals where the system depends on compensation rather than design.

Effort Concentration: Where the System Borrows Energy

Effort concentration shows where the system relies on people rather than on structure. In well-designed environments, effort is distributed predictably. Ownership is clear. Exceptions remain rare. When effort concentrates, stability depends on specific individuals or teams absorbing complexity that others cannot carry. Leaders often misread this as reliability. The same people "step up." Certain teams "always make it work." In reality, the system is borrowing energy to cover design gaps. Effort concentration reveals where endurance has replaced structure.

Where Effort Pools Instead of Spreading

Leaders usually know where effort concentrates. They just have not treated it as evidence.

Pay attention to:

Exception gravity
- The same people are repeatedly asked to support problems.
- Roles that absorb ambiguity others avoid.
- Teams that stabilize work without authority to change it.

Context dependency
- Individuals who carry knowledge no one else has.
- Work that only moves when specific people intervene.
- Coverage plans that quietly assume heroics.

Invisible load

- Calendars dominated by unplanned problem-solving.
- Interruptions that fragment focus.
- Work that advances only after personal rescue.

These patterns show up clearly in:

- Escalation paths that always land on the same names.
- Backlogs that move only after intervention.
- Handoffs that default to informal coordination.
- Projects that depend on presence rather than process.

Ask yourself: *Where does work go when the system cannot carry it on its own?*

What to Pay Attention to Without Adding Overhead

Effort concentration becomes visible through simple observation.

Examples leaders can examine regularly:

- Frequency of exceptions handled by the same roles.
- Distribution of interruptions across teams.
- Reliance on specific individuals to unblock work.
- Repetition of the same stabilizing behaviors.

When effort concentrates, recovery disappears for the people carrying it. The system appears resilient. The cost accumulates silently.

The Smallest Structural Shift That Redistributes Effort

When leaders notice effort concentration, the instinct is to reward endurance. That response validates the behavior. It leaves the structure unchanged. What reduces concentration is removing dependency.

A practical intervention sequence:

> **Name the dependency**
> - Where does work consistently detour?
> - What knowledge or authority is being borrowed?

> **Stabilize the handoff**
> - Clarify ownership where work routinely escalates.
> - Make decision rights explicit.

> **Design for absence**
> - Ask what would fail if this person were unavailable.
> - Adjust the structure so work can proceed.

> **Allow friction to surface**
> - Resist rescuing too quickly.
> - Let the system reveal where redesign is required.

Removing a dependency changes effort distribution more than recognition ever will.

Why This Changes the Feel of Work Quickly

Effort concentration creates invisible overload. It fragments attention. It accelerates burnout for a few. It hides fragility behind heroics. When effort redistributes, recovery returns. Judgment spreads. Stability improves without increasing oversight or headcount.

In operational environments under sustained pressure, the concentration of effort is one of the clearest indicators that the system is compensating for structural gaps. Addressing it often improves throughput while reducing individual strain.

From Seeing to Sustaining

By this point, the work has spoken. Leaders who learn to observe decision friction, completion integrity, and effort concentration no longer need to speculate about how work feels. The evidence is visible in how decisions move, how work closes, and where effort accumulates. Measurement has done its job when leaders can see strain forming early and identify the design choices driving it. But observation alone does not change the system.

If leaders notice friction and do nothing, the work teaches people a different lesson. It teaches them that visibility does not lead to redesign. It teaches them to keep compensating quietly. Over time, even careful measurement loses credibility if it does not result in structural change. This is where most organizations stall.

They see the patterns. They acknowledge the strain. They name the issues in meetings. Then the rhythm of work continues unchanged. People adapt again. Leaders grow accustomed to the cost. Measurement becomes descriptive rather than corrective. The difference between insight and impact is repetition.

Design changes must show up more than once to matter. They must reappear under pressure. They must survive the absence of leadership, competing priorities, and time. That requires cadence.

The final chapter focuses on how leaders embed what they have learned into the organization's operating rhythm.

- How observation becomes routine.
- How adjustments hold without constant attention.
- How reinforcement stops depending on memory or heroics.

Measurement shows leaders where the work is asking too much of them. Cadence determines whether that knowledge changes anything.

Chapter 10 is about making purpose durable by ensuring that what matters returns, reliably, through the rhythm of work itself.

CHAPTER 10
Turning the Words Into the Work

Why Leaders Measure the Wrong Things

People do not come to work hoping to disengage.

They come wanting to contribute, to matter, and to see their effort lead somewhere meaningful. We're not predisposed to be apathetic. It is a learned response. It takes hold when people repeatedly experience that caring costs more than it returns.

Most organizations do not fail to define purpose. They fail to operationalize it. The words exist. The intent is genuine. Leaders can explain the motto and defend its importance. Yet inside the work, hesitation grows. Decisions feel disconnected. Trade-offs feel inconsistent. Effort feels heavier than it should.

This is the final gap.

Turning a motto into lived experience requires moving purpose from language to mechanics. Into how priorities are revisited. Into how decisions are evaluated under pressure. Into how effort is reinforced, protected, and sustained. When those mechanics align, purpose no longer requires interpretation. It becomes visible through how work behaves.

Where Mottos Break Under Pressure

Most mottos fail in the same way. They operate at the level of belief, while the work operates at the level of survival. People may agree with the words. An agreement does not help when demands collide. When pressure rises and trade-offs must be made quickly, people rely on what the system has taught them to keep them safe.

Over time, people stop attempting to reconcile the motto with the work. They adapt. What leaders often describe as disengagement is frequently a rational response to a system that rewards self-protection.

Accountability Lives in Cadence

At this point in the book, one conclusion should be unavoidable. Purpose does not fail because leaders lack conviction. It fails because reinforcement lacks rhythm. Cadence is how accountability becomes structural.

Cadence determines what reappears in leadership attention. What reappears gets reinforced. What does not waft, regardless of stated importance. This is where leadership presence becomes leadership design.

• • •

Weekly rhythms determine what gets traction.
Monthly rhythms determine what gets negotiated.
Quarterly rhythms determine what gets deferred.

• • •

The question is whether those rhythms reinforce the purpose leaders claim to value or quietly undermine it.

Designing a Rhythm That Holds

There is no universal cadence. The proper rhythm reflects the nature of the work, the volatility of demand, and the cost of misalignment. Leaders lose effectiveness when they copy routines rather than design them.

A more useful starting question is simple:

What cannot be allowed to waiver?

In most organizations, the answer includes:

- Priority clarity when capacity tightens.
- Decision standards when trade-offs surface.
- Visibility into where effort concentrates.
- Recovery after sustained intensity.

Cadence exists to surface these before they turn into damage.

A practical rhythm looks like this:

> **Weekly**
>
> - Leaders examine movement.
> - Where did work slow unexpectedly? What required escalation or rescue? What decisions failed to translate into action?

> **Monthly**
>
> - Leaders examine reinforcement.
> - Which priorities held? Which standards bent? Where did people compensate to keep work moving?

Quarterly
- Leaders examine sustainability.
- Where did effort accumulate disproportionately? Where did energy fail to return? Which patterns repeated without correction?

Consistency Is the Work of Leadership

Leaders often associate accountability with follow-up, inspection, or intervention. In practice, accountability is expressed through what remains stable over time. People observe which priorities persist, which standards survive pressure, and which decisions remain intact once attention moves elsewhere.

When the same conditions produce different outcomes without explanation, people adapt defensively. When conditions produce consistent outcomes, people respond differently. They invest effort because the environment no longer introduces unnecessary uncertainty.

Leadership failure rarely comes from a lack of care. It comes from the inconsistency that teaches people to protect themselves. Accountability restores momentum by making the system predictable enough to trust.

When Purpose Stops Requiring Interpretation

There is a clear shift when purpose finally enters the work. People stop asking how to apply the motto. Decisions make sense. What returns is not enthusiasm. It is confidence.

* * *

Confidence that effort will not be wasted.
Confidence that judgment will not be penalized.
Confidence that the system will carry its share of the load.

* * *

This is what it looks like when a motto becomes operational.

CONCLUSION:
The Promise That Replaced the Smile

Recently, I had the chance to revisit the site of that childhood diner. The cracked vinyl booths were gone. The familiar sign was gone. In its place stood a Silver Diner.

I do not know why the original diner closed. I do not know whether it failed financially, changed hands, or simply faded out. I do wonder whether the issue was not demand, but follow-through. Whether the problem was not the promise, but the lack of discipline required to sustain it.

When I sat down, I noticed a card on the table.

It read:

Then the work did exactly what the card said it would do. The service was prompt and delivered with a smile. The order was accurate. The restaurant was clean. None of it felt accidental. The promise showed through the way work operated.

In that moment, the lesson became undeniable.

The Silver Diner's success wasn't because it had better words. It succeeded because it designed the work to support the promise. Someone made decisions about pace, quality, cleanliness, staffing, and standards. Someone built routines that reinforced those decisions. Someone chose to carry the promise through mechanics rather than messaging.

That choice replaced the diner I remembered. Organizations face the same risk.

Customers and employees walk in the door because of what you say. They stay, or leave, because of how the work treats them once they are inside. When promises remain aspirational, someone else eventually earns the right to make them operational. That replacement does not require innovation. It requires discipline.

This book exists for one reason.

Words get people in the door. Work determines whether they stay. If you want your purpose to matter, it must survive pressure. It must show up in decisions, trade-offs, routines, and recovery. It must repeat often enough that people stop questioning it.

Someone else is always willing to do that work.
The only question is whether it will be you.

APPENDIX

This appendix turns the book into action.

You already understand the core idea: purpose holds when work reinforces it. This section gives you tools to see where the system supports that promise and where people compensate to survive it.

Use this appendix like a reference, not a chapter. Start with the problem you feel in the work:

- Decisions stall or escalate.
- Work never finishes cleanly.
- Effort concentrates on the same few people.
- Engagement seems to be at risk.

Pick one tool that matches the pattern. Run it on real work, not opinions. Write down what repeats. Then make one structural change and hold it long enough for people to experience it as predictable.

Do not add programs. Do not launch a survey. Do not try to fix everything.

Your goal: reduce the effort people spend interpreting the system so they can invest that energy in judgment, quality, and momentum.

Best next step: choose one tool, run it this week, and commit to one rule you will enforce for 60 days.

RHYTHM Operating System

A practical model for turning purpose into daily experience

RHYTHM is an operating system for leadership. It explains how purpose becomes real through repeated decisions, visible standards, and predictable patterns of work.

When any part weakens, effort increases and energy drops. When all six work together, clarity holds, judgment improves, and momentum sustains.

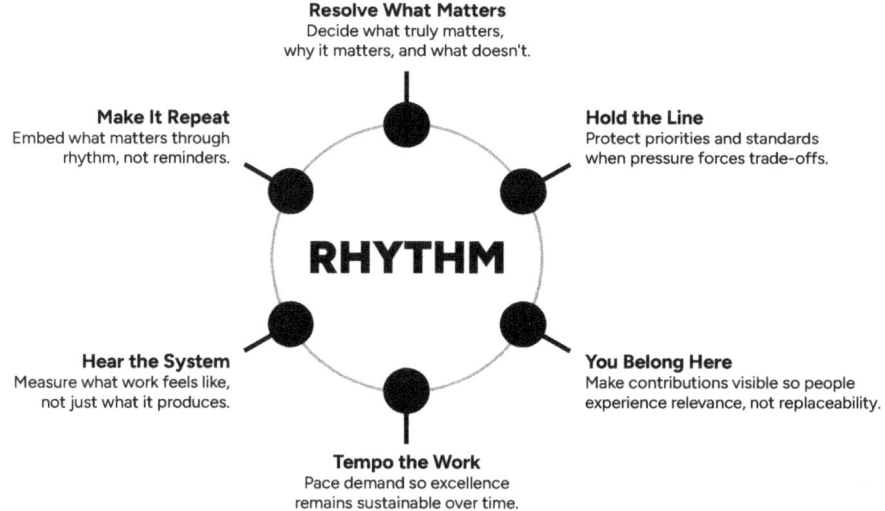

How the System Works

RHYTHM is not a checklist.

It is a loop.
- **Clarity** sets direction
- **Intentionality** protects it
- **Connection** sustains commitment
- **Recovery** preserves judgment
- **Measurement** reveals reality
- **Cadence** makes it repeat

Break the rhythm and people compensate.

Hold the rhythm, and behavior stabilizes.

Why Satisfaction Is Not Engagement

And why confusing them drains energy without leaders realizing it

Leaders often believe they have an engagement problem when, in reality, they have a definition problem. For decades, research has drawn a clear distinction between job satisfaction and employee engagement. In practice, organizations blur that line. They optimize for comfort, then wonder why commitment fails to follow.

That confusion produces a predictable pattern: employees stay, but they stop investing.

Job satisfaction is about conditions

Job satisfaction refers to how people evaluate their jobs and their work environments. Edwin Locke's foundational work defines it as a positive emotional state resulting from the appraisal of one's job or job experiences.[8]

Satisfaction rises when:
- Pay feels fair
- Schedules feel manageable

- Tools and policies reduce friction
- The environment feels stable and predictable

Satisfaction matters. Research consistently links it to retention and morale. But satisfaction is attitudinal, not behavioral. It reflects how people feel about work, not how deeply they invest in it. A satisfied employee can still withhold judgment, initiative, and discretionary effort.

Engagement is about investment

Employee engagement describes how fully people bring themselves to their work. William Kahn's seminal research frames engagement as the extent to which individuals draw on their cognitive, emotional, and physical selves in role performance.[5]

Engagement rises when people experience meaning, safety, and the ability to contribute without constant self-protection.

Engagement shows up as:
- Persistence under pressure
- Attention to quality
- Willingness to use judgment
- Care for outcomes beyond minimum requirements

Engagement is not a mood. It is a choice people make repeatedly based on how work responds to their effort.

The performance difference matters

Large-scale meta-analytic research confirms what leaders observe anecdotally. Engagement predicts performance outcomes more strongly and more consistently than satisfaction alone.

The Gallup research team's meta-analysis across hundreds of business units found that higher engagement correlates with stronger productivity, profitability, customer outcomes, safety, and quality.[9] Satisfaction alone does not explain those results.

That distinction explains a common leadership frustration:
- Teams report being "fine"
- Surveys look acceptable
- Yet ownership, urgency, and pride fade

Comfort is present. Commitment is not.

The leadership mistake

Leaders often try to solve engagement problems with satisfaction tools. They add benefits, adjust perks, or improve communication while leaving the work design unchanged. When priorities stay ambiguous, standards bend under pressure, and effort goes unseen, engagement erodes even in comfortable environments.

Engagement responds to how work operates, not how it is marketed.

The practical implication

Satisfaction sets the floor.
Engagement determines the ceiling.

Leaders should:
- Use satisfaction data to diagnose conditions and fairness
- Use engagement signals to diagnose meaning, agency, and sustainability

Treating them as interchangeable weakens both.

A Manager's Reference:
Staying Connected at Work

Employees are constantly forming opinions about their work. They rarely say them directly. Most disengagement shows up after the answers to these questions turn negative. Your job is not to ask them all at once. Your job is to notice them early and respond consistently.

The Four Questions Employees Are Always Asking

1. What do I get?
What they're really checking:
Is this fair and predictable?

They're watching:
- Workload vs. expectations
- How consistently rules apply
- Whether time and effort are respected

You should watch for:
- Confusion about priorities or process
- Quiet frustration about "how things really work"
- Pulling back from extra effort

Ask:
- "What feels harder than it should right now?"
- "Where do expectations feel unclear?"

2. What can I give?

What they're really checking:
Does my effort actually matter?

They're testing:
- Whether judgment is welcome
- Whether initiative helps or hurts
- Whether ideas lead to action

You should watch for:
- Hesitation to take initiative
- Over-reliance on approval
- "Just tell me what you want" behavior

Ask:
- "Where do you feel underused?"
- "What would you change if you had more room?"

3. Do I belong?

What they're really checking:
Am I valued here beyond my output?

They're paying attention to:
- How people are treated under pressure
- Who gets exceptions
- Whether input gets ignored once pressure increases

You should watch for:
- Silence in meetings
- Withdrawal during stressful periods
- Defensive or emotionally distant behavior

Ask:
- "When things get hectic, what's hardest about being here?"
- "Where do you feel supported? Where don't you?"

4. How can we grow?

What they're really checking:

Is there a future here that includes me?

Growth includes:
- Skills
- Trust
- Exposure
- Challenge

Not just promotions.

You should watch for:
- Plateaued performance
- Reduced curiosity
- Talking about growth only outside the team

Ask:
- "What do you want more of in the next few months?"
- "What would make this role more interesting?"

When These Questions Surface Most

Upon hire or role change

Most active questions:
- What do I get?
- What can I give?

Focus: Set expectations clearly and explain how contributions work.

During regular 1:1s

Most active questions:
- What can I give?
- Do I belong?

Focus: Remove friction, reinforce trust, protect dignity.

At milestones (projects, anniversaries, transitions)

Most active questions:

- Do I belong?
- How can we grow?

Focus: Acknowledge contribution and clarify what's next.

Turning Listening Into Action

Listening without follow-through breaks trust. Look for patterns across conversations.

When patterns show up, adjust something real:
- Clarify priorities
- Reset workload
- Make their contribution visible
- Open growth paths earlier

Small changes matter more than perfect answers.

Manager Reality Check

If you only hear these answers in:
- Surveys
- Exit interviews
- Escalations

You're already late. Employees don't disengage suddenly. They disengage quietly, one unanswered question at a time.

The Bottom Line

Employees are already answering these questions. Managers decide whether anyone hears them in time.

Mechanism Case Study:

Legacy Checks at Hershey

Let's break down the simple mechanics of the Legacy Checks in action and why the design translates beyond a single organization.

At its core, the Legacy Check system existed to solve one problem. Values only matter when people can recognize them in motion. The mechanism translated abstract language into visible, repeatable reinforcement inside daily work.

Every manager carried a small checkbook. Each check included space for the employee's name, the date, and the organization's four values: Own, Anticipate, Delight, Inspire. Issuing a check required real-time observation. A manager had to witness a specific behavior and document it immediately. Recognition was handwritten and precise. It named what happened and tied it directly to a value.

That constraint mattered. Writing forced clarity. A manager could not rely on generic praise or vague encouragement. They had to identify an action, explain why it mattered, and connect it to a shared standard. Over time, this sharpened attention. Values stopped functioning as reminders and began functioning as lenses through which work was seen and evaluated.

Each check generated three copies. One copy went directly to the employee at the moment of recognition. One copy went to the employee's manager to ensure reinforcement extended beyond the initial interaction.

The third copy carried redeemable value. Employees could exchange it for experiences across the Hershey destination, including dining, park access, and events. The value increased incrementally and cycled ($5, $10, $15, and $20), which reinforced steady participation rather than one-time accumulation.

Visibility completed the loop. In many teams, checks were displayed in shared spaces. Recognition became social rather than private. Employees could see which behaviors earned reinforcement and how often they appeared. Patterns emerged naturally. People learned what ownership, anticipation, delight, and inspiration looked like by watching those values unfold in real-world examples.

The system depended on discipline rather than scale. Managers had to notice behavior consistently. They had to write clearly. They had to reinforce the same values every time. Recognition lived inside the flow of work instead of waiting for quarterly reviews or annual cycles.

What makes this mechanism transferable is not the check's format. It is the structure underneath it.

Every organization already recognizes people in some way. The question is whether recognition teaches anything repeatable.

The Legacy Check worked because it met five conditions that apply universally:

1. Recognition happened close to the behavior.
2. Recognition required specificity rather than sentiment.
3. Recognition reinforced a small, consistent set of values.
4. Recognition was visible beyond the individual moment.
5. Recognition carried meaning that extended beyond praise.

These conditions hold regardless of the environment.

In remote and distributed teams, the artifact changes while the mechanics remain. A digital card, a shared channel post, a short written note, or a lightweight workflow inside existing tools can serve the same purpose. What matters is not the medium.

What matters is that leaders observe real work, document what they see, connect it to shared values, and make the reinforcement visible to others.

Distributed work reduces incidental observation. That makes intentional reinforcement more important, not less. When recognition becomes deliberate, remote teams gain clarity rather than lose it. People understand what "good" looks like even when they are not physically together.

The Legacy Check worked because the system reduced the effort required to live the values. It embedded reinforcement into daily work so people did not have to remember what mattered. The mechanism carried that burden for them.

When reinforcement happens consistently, close to the behavior, and tied to shared standards, belief stabilizes. People stop guessing. They stop translating language into action on their own. The work demonstrates what earns attention and why.

That is the opportunity every organization has. Design a mechanism that teaches values through repeated experience rather than explanation. The artifact will differ. The discipline will not.

The First 90 Days

A guided checklist with space to think, notice, and decide

Leadership problems often begin with speed. Work changes before it is understood.

This tool slows the right things down and moves the right things forward. Use it in order. Do not rush it. Write things down. What you notice matters as much as what you change.

Days 1–30: See the Work Clearly

Your focus this month:
Understanding how work actually behaves for your team.

You are not fixing yet. You are paying attention to where effort flows, where it hesitates, and where it quietly drains.

Weekly self-check:
- ☐ I slowed my response time
- ☐ I listened without explaining or correcting
- ☐ I captured patterns instead of isolated issues

What felt hardest about not acting right away?

What to watch for (daily, informal)

1. Decision hesitation

(This is when people pause, double-check, or escalate routine decisions.)

Where did I notice hesitation most often?

What do people seem unsure will hold?

2. Work that never quite finishes

(These are the tasks or projects stay open longer than expected.)

What work keeps reappearing without closure?

What does "done" seem to mean in practice right now?

3. Effort concentrating on the same people
(Who are the few individuals that regularly step in to save or smooth work?)

Who absorbs friction most often?

What would slow down if they stepped back?

One leadership team conversation (by the end of the month)

Ask this question and write down what you hear:
"Where does work feel harder than it needs to right now?"

Repeated themes I heard:

Conversation self-check:

☐ I captured answers without debating

☐ I resisted solving anything yet

What surprised me most during this month?

Days 31–60: Fix One Thing That Keeps Repeating

Your focus this month:
Removing one recurring source of friction.

You are narrowing the field. One change. One place. One clear shift.

Select one fix to focus on:
- ☐ Decisions stall or reopen
- ☐ Work stays open across cycles
- ☐ The same people carry extra load

Why this one stood out:

- ☐ I committed to focusing on only this

Write one rule that changes how work moves.

My rule:

Rule self-check:
- ☐ The rule is short
- ☐ The rule is easy to remember
- ☐ The rule stands without explanation

What behavior this rule is meant to protect:

Hold the rule under pressure:
- ☐ I applied the rule consistently
- ☐ I noticed where it felt uncomfortable
- ☐ I avoided bending it quietly

When was it hardest to hold the rule?

What happened when I did hold it?

What I observed changing:
- ☐ Fewer follow-ups
- ☐ Less second-guessing
- ☐ Clearer movement

Where did stability start to show up?

Days 61–90: Make the Pattern Repeat

Your focus this month:

Helping the work reinforce the right behavior on its own.

This is about predictability. People should know what will be asked, where, and why.

Select 3-4 weekly questions and keep them consistent. Things to consider include:

- ☐ What mattered most this week?
- ☐ What slowed us down?
- ☐ What finished cleanly?
- ☐ Where did someone prevent a problem?

Our weekly questions:

1.
2.
3.
4.

Why these questions matter right now:

Decide where they live
- ☐ We use meetings we already have
- ☐ We ask them in the same place every week

Where these questions show up:

Decide on your responses before pressure hits.

Complete these sentences:

- When priorities conflict, we will

- When work spills over, we will

- When overload shows up repeatedly, we will

What feels hardest about these commitments:

Run the rhythm for a full month:
- ☐ We kept the questions steady
- ☐ We avoided adding tools or processes
- ☐ We let repetition do the work

What changed because things stayed consistent:

What to Leave Out of the First 90 Days

Pause before adding any of these:
- ☐ Engagement surveys
- ☐ Motivational messaging
- ☐ Value or mission rewrites
- ☐ Broad transformation efforts

What I felt tempted to add anyway:

Ninety-Day Reflection

At the end of ninety days, answer honestly.
- ☐ Do people hesitate less?
- ☐ Does work finish more often?
- ☐ Does less depend on a few individuals?
- ☐ Do I intervene less than before?

What feels more stable now:

What still needs attention next:

Purpose shows up when work grows more reliable. That reliability starts with how leaders pay attention, what they protect, and what they make repeat.

Rating Scales Explained

Several tools in this appendix use a 1–5 rating scale. This scale exists to give everyone a shared way to describe patterns they already experience.

Use the same meaning for each number every time.

1 – Strongly disagree
This almost never happens. The system actively works against it.

2 – Disagree
This happens occasionally, but not reliably.

3 – Neutral or inconsistent
It depends on the leader, the team, or the situation.

4 – Agree
This happens often enough that people can rely on it.

5 – Strongly agree
This happens consistently, even when things get hard.

Important rule
Rate what happens repeatedly in real work. Do not rate intent, values, or isolated examples.

Purpose Reality Check

This exercise shows where purpose is reinforced by how work is designed and where it survives only because leaders personally intervene.

When to use it:
- Before launching a major initiative
- After a reorganization, acquisition, or leadership change
- When results look fine, but energy, confidence, or judgment is slipping

Time: 10–15 minutes

Materials:
- Printed copies (or a shared doc)
- Pen or notes app
- A timer

Setup: Everyone completes the ratings silently and individually first. This matters. Independent scoring surfaces fundamental differences in experience before group discussion smooths them over.

How to Run the Exercise

Step 1: Set the rule

- Read this aloud:

  "Score what happens often, not what we wish were true."

- No discussion yet.

Step 2: Rate each statement

- Rate each statement from 1 to 5 using the scale above.
- Do not explain your ratings. Do not compare scores yet.

Step 3: Identify weak spots

- Circle your three lowest-rated statements.
- These are the places where the system is most likely to ask people to compensate.

Step 4: Compare scores as a group

- For each statement, capture three numbers:
  - The average score
  - The highest score
  - The lowest score
- Do this quickly. You are looking for patterns, not debate.

Step 5: Name misalignment

- Any statement with a spread of two points or more (for example, a 2 and a 4) indicates a shared problem experienced very differently across the group.

Rate each statement from 1 (Strongly Disagree) to 5 (Strongly Agree).

Clarity

1. Most people can name the top priority right now without asking or checking.
2. When priorities conflict, people know which one takes precedence.
3. Leaders can clearly say what work would slow down or stop under pressure.

Intentionality

4. We uphold our standards even when the outcome is at risk.
5. Exceptions are named openly instead of handled quietly.
6. High performers are held to the same behavioral standards as everyone else.

Connection

7. People understand how their work contributes beyond output.
8. Essential behind-the-scenes work is recognized before something breaks.
9. Respect here is not earned through overwork or constant availability.

Recovery

10. Work reaches clear finish points rather than lingering unfinished.
11. Urgency is occasional, not constant.
12. People end most days with energy to continue, not just relief that the day is over.

Scoring and interpretation:

Add all twelve scores together.

- 48–60

    Purpose is reinforced by how work is designed.

    36–47

- Purpose holds inconsistently. Leaders are compensating manually

    Below 36

    The system trains people to protect themselves.

Output:

At the end of the exercise, produce two things:

1. A ranked list of the top three system weaknesses
2. One decision: Which single weakness will we redesign first?

Do not try to fix everything. One structural change done well will matter more than three discussed abstractly.

What Breaks First Trade-Off Map

Instead of relying on judgment in the moment, leaders should decide in advance what gives way when capacity tightens. That decision is what creates clarity for teams under pressure. If leaders do not make these choices explicitly, teams will make them quietly.

When to use it:
- During planning cycles or roadmap reviews
- When demand is increasing, but capacity is not
- Before launching a new initiative without removing old ones

Time: 20–30 minutes

Materials:
- A whiteboard or shared document
- A list of active initiatives, commitments, or priorities
- A timer

Setup: This tool works only if leaders are willing to make trade-offs visible. Bring real work into the room. If priorities stay abstract, the exercise will stall.

How to Run the Exercise

Step 1: List protected commitments

As a group, list 3–5 commitments that must hold even under pressure. These are the things you will protect at the expense of other work.

Examples:
- Regulatory obligations
- Core operational stability
- Safety, quality, or trust requirements

Do not debate wording at this phase. Focus on what cannot break.

Step 2: List variable commitments

Next, list 5–10 important but negotiable commitments. These are priorities that matter but could slow, pause, or stop if required.

Examples:
- Internal improvement projects
- Experimental initiatives
- Nice-to-have enhancements
- Work with flexible timelines

If leaders struggle here, it signals that everything is being treated as critical.

Step 3: Apply pressure scenarios

Pressure can take many forms. Demand increase is among the most common, which is why this tool starts there. You can substitute other pressures if they better reflect your reality.

Common pressure types include:
- Demand increases or spikes
- Demand drops suddenly
- Headcount reductions or hiring freezes
- Budget cuts
- Regulatory or compliance changes
- Major customer escalations
- Technology failures or system instability

For this exercise, start with a demand increase unless another pressure is more urgent right now.

If demand increases by...	Work that slows, pauses, or stops	Work that stays protected	The rule teams should follow
10%			
20%			
30%			

Rules that keep this honest
- "We'll work harder" is not an acceptable answer.
- If everything stays protected, clarity does not exist.
- If leaders cannot agree, teams cannot guess correctly.

Discomfort here means the exercise is working.

Step 4: Write the operating rule

For each row, complete this sentence:

"When demand increases by ___%, teams should _____ first."

This is the sentence teams will use when priorities collide. If you cannot write it clearly, the system will default to escalation or self-protection.

Interpreting the results:

Use the table to pressure-test leadership clarity.

Warning signs
- Leaders protect everything at 10% pressure.
- Trade-offs only appear in extreme scenarios.
- Different leaders argue for other protections.

These explain why teams hesitate, escalate, or mitigate risk.

Output:

This tool must produce a single, shareable artifact:

"When pressure rises, here's what changes first."

That artifact should:
- Name what slows or stops
- Name what stays protected
- Remove ambiguity before pressure arrives

Publish it. Revisit it quarterly. Adjust it deliberately.

Reinforcement Audit

This exercise reveals what the organization actually reinforces when pressure shows up. Not what leaders say matters. Not what policies intend. What repeated leadership responses teach people about how to succeed here. Over time, those responses become the fundamental operating rules.

When to use it:
- After a high-pressure period or major push
- After a missed target or significant escalation
- Before performance, promotion, or compensation decisions
- When teams seem cautious, political, or disengaged

Time required: 20 minutes

Materials:
- Calendar covering the last 30 days
- Notes from leadership meetings, escalations, or reviews
- Sticky notes or a shared document

Setup:

This exercise works only when the conversation stays grounded in reality. The goal is to surface what repeated leadership responses teach people about how work really operates.

Use these guardrails:
- Assume positive intent from everyone involved.
- Focus on observable actions and outcomes, not motivations.
- Describe what someone watching the work unfold would reasonably conclude.
- Notice discomfort without trying to smooth it away.

If the discussion slides into explanations or defense, pause and return to this question:

"If this response happened again and again, what would people learn from it?"

How to Run the Exercise

Step 1: Set the review window

Agree on the time period you are reviewing.

As a default, use the last 30 days. If there was a major event, anchor the review to that period instead.

Step 2: Identify pressure moments

Individually list moments where standards were tested.

Examples include:
- Deadlines slipping
- Quality issues surfacing
- Customer escalations
- A high performer creating friction
- Competing priorities colliding

Write down specific situations, not general impressions.

Step 3: Audit what actually happened

For each pressure moment, answer the questions below in writing. Do not explain why decisions were made. Record what the outcome would reasonably teach someone watching the work.

Audit questions
- Which behaviors were rewarded, explicitly or implicitly, because they produced results?
- Where did leaders override an agreed standard to keep things moving?
- Where did speed or convenience take priority without an explicit trade-off decision?
- Which exceptions were made without being clearly named as exceptions?
- Where did leaders step in to absorb friction instead of letting the system feel it?

If you struggle to answer a question, that absence is data.

Step 4: Name the pattern

Review your answers and complete this sentence as a group:

"When things get uncomfortable, we tend to reinforce _____, even though we say _____ matters more."

Use concrete language. Avoid values or slogans.

Step 5: Choose one line to hold

You cannot change reinforcement everywhere at once. Choose one standard that will hold for the next 60 days, even if it slows progress or creates tension. Write it as a rule:

"For the next 60 days, we will not _____, even if _____."

Interpreting the results:

Pay attention to repetition.

Warning signs include:
- Exceptions appear frequently but are rarely discussed
- High performers receive different treatment
- Leaders repeatedly step in to smooth over friction
- Outcomes matter more than how they were achieved

Output:

This exercise must produce one clear decision:

A single standard that will be enforced consistently for the next 60 days. Do not announce it broadly yet. Let people experience it through consistent leadership response.

Contribution Visibility Map

This exercise reveals which work the organization depends on but rarely sees. It helps leaders identify where contributions disappear into the system and redesign how they become visible.

When to use it:
- When engagement feels flat without a clear cause
- When specific teams feel "always on" or taken for granted
- When recognition feels uneven or performative
- When work only gets attention after something breaks

Time: 25–40 minutes

Materials:
- A list of roles or teams
- A whiteboard or shared document
- A timer

Setup:
This exercise requires leaders and operators in the room. Do not run it with executives only. Contribution becomes invisible when the distance from the work grows.

Set this expectation before starting:

"We are mapping how contribution actually shows up today, not how we intend to recognize it."

Focus on how work is experienced, not how recognition is designed on paper.

How to Run the Exercise

Step 1: List roles or teams

As a group, list the primary roles or teams involved in delivering work. Do not overthink this. Capture the roles people depend on most often.

Examples:
- Frontline teams
- Support functions
- Technical or operational specialists
- Coordinators, planners, or quality roles

Step 2: Map contribution by role

For each role or team, answer the questions below in writing. Avoid praise language. Focus on consequences.

Contribution questions
- What problem would appear if this work stopped for a week?
- How would anyone notice?
- When was this contribution last named publicly or in a leadership forum?

Capture short, concrete answers.

Step 3: Identify invisible essentials

Review your answers and mark the roles where:
- Failure would be obvious
- Success is quiet or taken for granted
- Attention arrives mainly when something goes wrong

These are your invisible essential contributions. They carry risk and effort without corresponding visibility.

Step 4: Design visibility inside the work

Choose a straightforward mechanism to make this contribution visible before failure occurs.

Good mechanisms share three traits:
- They happen close to the work
- They name specific actions, not general effort
- They repeat predictably

Examples:
- A standing agenda item highlighting "work that prevented a problem."
- A rotating spotlight on behind-the-scenes contributions in ops reviews
- A lightweight recognition artifact tied to clear standards or values

Do not design a program. Design a repeatable moment.

Interpreting the results:

The following conditions weaken connection even when performance remains consistent.

Warning signs include:
- Critical roles are only mentioned after failures
- Recognition favors visible effort over stabilizing work
- The same teams absorb risk quietly
- People describe their value defensively rather than confidently

Output:

This activity must produce two things:
1. A short list of invisible essential contributions
2. One concrete mechanism that will make those contributions visible every week

If visibility depends on memory or goodwill, it will fade. If visibility is built into the rhythm of work, connection strengthens.

Completion Integrity Check

This exercise helps you identify work that never fully finishes and fix one example.

When to use it:
- When everything feels "in progress"
- When initiatives restart more often than they finish
- When teams complain about constant reprioritization
- When people feel busy but not accomplished

Time: 20–30 minutes

Materials:
- A current list of initiatives, projects, or priorities
- A recent status report or backlog view
- A shared document or whiteboard

Setup:

This exercise focuses on how work moves, not on how hard people work. Do not frame this as a productivity discussion. Focus on whether the system creates closure or perpetual motion.

Set this expectation before starting: *"We are looking for where work lingers, not who is slow."*

How to Run the Exercise

Step 1: Identify carryover work

As a group, list initiatives or commitments that:
- Have remained active longer than planned
- Reappear unchanged across multiple reviews
- Are described as "almost done" repeatedly

Do not explain why. Just list them.

Step 2: Select one initiative to repair

Choose one active initiative to examine closely. Pick something representative, not the biggest or most politically charged item.

Step 3: Define "done" precisely

For the selected initiative, answer the questions below in writing. Be concrete. Avoid aspirational language.
- Done means: What specific condition signals completion?
- Done does not require: What usually gets added late but is not essential?
- Ownership releases when: At what point does responsibility officially end?

If "done" cannot be described clearly, completion is not possible.

Step 4: Protect the finish

Write a simple rule that blocks scope creep: "No new work is added to this initiative until the defined 'done' condition is met." Decide who enforces this rule and where it is reinforced.

Step 5: Create a closure moment

Design a lightweight, repeatable way to mark completion.

Examples:
- A brief demo or walkthrough
- A short written recap of what changed
- A confirmation sent to affected teams or customers

Interpreting the results:

These patterns explain fatigue even when the workload seems reasonable.

Warning signs
- "Done" is described vaguely or changes frequently
- Teams carry context from old work into new initiatives
- People struggle to name recent finishes

Output:

This exercise must produce one concrete artifact: A clear definition of done, a rule that protects it, and a visible closure step.

Use this as a template for other initiatives.

Completion restores energy by allowing attention to release. Without it, recovery never enters the work.

Effort Concentration Heatmap

This exercise shows where effort keeps landing on the same people instead of being carried by the system. It helps you see where progress depends on intervention rather than design and identify one place where work relies on personal rescue.

The aim is not to reduce effort, but to stop borrowing it from the same roles over and over again.

When to use it:
- When burnout clusters around a few people
- When the same names appear in escalations repeatedly
- When progress depends on who is available, not how work is designed
- When people are praised for "stepping up" too often

Time: 25 minutes

Materials:
- Escalation notes, logs, or informal records
- Calendars from the last two weeks
- A shared document or whiteboard

Setup:

This activity examines where work goes when the system cannot carry it on its own. Focus on roles and patterns, not personalities.

Set this expectation before starting:

"We are mapping where effort concentrates, not who works the hardest."

How to Run the Exercise

Step 1: Name the stabilizers

As a group, list the people or roles that:

- Get pulled into problems unexpectedly
- Are asked to "take a quick look" or "help unblock things".
- Appear repeatedly in escalations or urgent meetings.

List names or roles only. Do not explain why they are involved.

Step 2: Map the pull

For each person or role listed, answer the questions below in writing. Be specific. Avoid praise language.

- What types of problems end up here most often?
- What decision, handoff, or ownership gap causes that pull?
- What context or authority does this person provide that the system lacks?

If the same answers appear across multiple roles, you are seeing a design issue rather than an individual one.

Step 3: Run the absence test

For each stabilizer, answer this question:

"If this person or role were unavailable for two weeks, what would stop moving or break?"

Write the answer plainly. If progress stalls, effort is concentrated instead of distributed.

Step 4: Remove one dependency

Choose one recurring dependency to address now. Pick the smallest structural change that reduces reliance on a person.

Examples:
- Clarify the decision owner
- Redesign an escalation path
- Document critical context
- Change a handoff rule
- Allow a known friction point to surface instead of being absorbed.

Write the change as a rule: *"Going forward, _____ will happen instead of relying on _____."* Decide who owns the change and where it will be reinforced.

Interpreting the results:

These patterns explain burnout even in high-performing teams.

Warning signs
- The same people keep getting pulled into very different problems.
- Things stall or fall apart when specific people are out.
- Critical information resides in people's heads rather than in the process or tools.
- Problems get solved because someone steps in, not because the system works.

Output:

This tool must produce one concrete result: One dependency removed and one rule changed, so work no longer relies on heroics.

Cadence Builder

This tool helps leaders design the operating rhythm that keeps everything else working. Clarity, standards, visibility, and completion fade when they rely on memory or emphasis.

Cadence removes that dependency by deciding in advance where critical behaviors are reinforced and how often. This is not a meeting framework. It is a way to design how decisions repeat.

When to use it:
- After redesigning priorities, standards, or workflows
- When improvements fade after early momentum
- When leaders feel stuck repeating the same messages
- When teams hesitate because expectations shift week to week

How to Use This Tool
This is a design exercise, not a facilitated activity.

Leaders should work through it together, commit to the result, and run it consistently for at least one quarter before making changes. Stability is part of the design.

The Cadence Principle

Every organization already runs on a cadence.

Meetings, reviews, and routines all teach people what matters, whether leaders intend them to or not. Cadence is already shaping behavior.

This tool helps leaders take control. If something important does not repeat on a predictable rhythm, it will be replaced by whatever does.

The Reinforcement Areas

Cadence exists to reinforce a small number of things that cannot drift. These reinforcement areas reflect the questions people are already asking through their behavior.

When leaders do not answer these questions consistently, teams fill in the gaps themselves.

Clarity

The question people are asking:
What matters right now, and what can wait?

Intentionality

The question people are asking:
What standards actually hold when trade-offs appear?

Connection

The question people are asking:

Does my contribution matter before something breaks?

Recovery

The question people are asking:

How does work finish, and when does pace get checked?

Designing the Cadence

For each reinforcement area, leaders must decide five things.

1. The forum

Where does this reinforcement area live?

Examples include:
- Weekly leadership or operations reviews
- Monthly performance or quality forums
- Quarterly planning sessions
- Team-level standups or retrospectives

Reuse existing forums whenever possible.

2. The frequency

How often must this reinforcement repeat to shape behavior?

- Weekly reinforces action and adjustment
- Monthly reinforces consistency and standards
- Quarterly reinforces sustainability and direction

If reinforcement happens less often than the work itself, it will lose.

3. The fixed question

What question gets asked every time, regardless of circumstances?

This question should remain stable. Changing it weakens the rhythm.

Examples:
- "What matters most this week, and what are we not doing?"
- "Where did we hold the line, and where did we bend it?"
- "What work prevented a problem or enabled progress?"
- "What finished cleanly, and what pressure is building?"

4. The decision owner

Who is responsible for acting on what surfaces?

Cadence without ownership becomes observation. Each forum needs a named owner with the authority to respond.

5. The action rule

What happens when a signal appears?

Every forum should define a simple rule:

"If we see _____, we will _____ within _____."

This turns cadence into consequence.

Example Cadence Map

Clarity

- Forum: Weekly leadership review
- Frequency: Weekly
- Fixed question: "What matters most this week, and what are we not doing?"
- Decision owner: Functional leader
- Action rule: If priorities conflict, one is paused within 24 hours.

Intentionality

- Forum: Monthly performance review
- Frequency: Monthly
- Fixed question: "Where did we hold standards under pressure?"
- Decision owner: Senior leader
- Action rule: If an exception appears, it is named and addressed within the month.

Connection

- Forum: Weekly team forum
- Frequency: Weekly
- Fixed question: "What work prevented failure or enabled progress?"
- Decision owner: Team lead
- Action rule: If contribution is invisible, it is named before the next cycle.

Recovery

- Forum: Monthly planning review
- Frequency: Monthly
- Fixed question: "What finished, and what pressure is building?"
- Decision owner: Operations or planning lead
- Action rule: If load exceeds capacity, work is removed before new work is added.

Common Cadence Failures

These failures explain why progress fades without obvious cause.

- Reinforcement depends on leader memory
- Questions change based on mood or crisis
- Conversations repeat without decisions
- Action rules exist but are never triggered

Output

This tool should produce a one-page cadence map that includes:

- Each reinforcement area
- The forum where it lives
- The frequency
- The fixed question
- The decision owner
- The action rule

Review this map quarterly. Do not revise it reactively.

ENDNOTES

1. John A. Bargh and Tanya L. Chartrand, "The Unbearable Automaticity of Being," *American Psychologist* 54, no. 7 (1999): 462–479.

2. Martha S. Feldman and Brian T. Pentland, "Reconceptualizing Organizational Routines as a Source of Flexibility and Change," *Administrative Science Quarterly* 48, no. 1 (2003): 94–118.

3. Karl E. Weick, *Sensemaking in Organizations* (Thousand Oaks, CA: Sage Publications, 1995).

4. Edgar H. Schein, *Organizational Culture and Leadership,* 5th ed. (Hoboken, NJ: John Wiley & Sons, 2017).

5. William A. Kahn, "Psychological Conditions of Personal Engagement and Disengagement at Work," *Academy of Management Journal* 33, no. 4 (1990): 692–724.

6. Christina Maslach and Michael P. Leiter, *The Truth About Burnout: How Organizations Cause Personal Stress and What to Do About It* (San Francisco: Jossey-Bass, 1997).

7. Sabine Sonnentag and Charlotte Fritz, "The Recovery Experience Questionnaire: Development and Validation of a Measure for Assessing Recuperation and Unwinding from Work," *Journal of Occupational Health Psychology* 12, no. 3 (2007): 204–221.

8. Edwin A. Locke, "The Nature and Causes of Job Satisfaction," in *Handbook of Industrial and Organizational Psychology,* ed. Marvin D. Dunnette (Chicago: Rand McNally, 1976), 1297–1349.

9. James K. Harter, Frank L. Schmidt, and Theodore L. Hayes, "Business-Unit-Level Relationship Between Employee Satisfaction, Employee Engagement, and Business Outcomes: A Meta-Analysis," *Journal of Applied Psychology* 87, no. 2 (2002): 268–279.

INDEX

A

accountability, 58–59, 81–82, 100–3
action and behavior
    aligning with words, 1–7, 57–59, 99–103, 105–7
    culture shaped by daily actions, 1–2, 24, 28–29, 33–35, 37–40
    everyday trade-offs, 35–37, 59–63, 140–44
    follow-through on promises, 7–8, 33–40, 57–60, 100–3, 105–7
activity vs. impact, 6–7, 54, 83–85, 94, 98
adjustment, structural. See design, structural
alignment
    accidental vs. intentional, 20–22, 33–35, 59–60
    between mottos and work, 1–3, 7–8, 57–60, 99–103
    between purpose and rhythm, 21–23, 54–55, 109–10
    between stated values and reinforcement, 28–29, 33–40, 63–67, 145–49
    team vs. leadership view, 2–4, 58–60, 83–86, 136–39
anxiety, 4, 44–45, 50–52, 88–89, 92–93

B

belonging. See connection; "You Belong Here" rhythm
belief
    exhausting belief without design, 8, 12–13, 55, 57–60, 99–100

belief vs. experience, 2–4, 19–21, 39–40, 57–60, 99–103
behavior
    consistent vs. inconsistent, 28–29, 33–40, 62–67, 145–49
    pattern ownership, 58–60, 80–82, 109–10
    teaching through systems, 3–4, 19–22, 28–29, 33–35, 59–60
burnout
    as system outcome, not personal failure, 14–16, 49–53
    and effort concentration, 52–53, 94–97, 158–61
    and always-on work, 49–52
    lagging indicator, 52–53
    top performers and burnout, 15–16, 52–53, 95–97

C

cadence
    as leadership mechanism, 23, 57–60, 80–82, 100–3, 162–68
cadence builder tool, 162–68
    memory vs. design, 80–82, 162–68
    weekly, monthly, quarterly rhythms, 80–82, 100–2, 162–68
care and caring
    unpredictable cost of caring, 3, 7–8, 11–13, 15–16, 41–47, 49–53
    caring vs. compensation, 11–13, 15–16, 49–53, 95–97

case studies and examples
    financial services system friction, 10–13
    Half Day Cafe (Mason, Ohio), 35–38
    Hershey Entertainment & Resorts and Legacy Checks, 46–47, 121–23
    manufacturing overtime standards, 65–67
    merger and belonging, 69–71
    percussionist and click track, 17–19
    Silver Diner promise, 105–7
    technology/SaaS sprint prioritization, 60–62
    contact center occupancy and pace, 74–76
climate of work. See work experience
clarity
    and ambiguity costs, 1–3, 25–27, 59–60, 83–87, 136–39
    and confusion vs. information, 25–27
    and decision boundaries, 29–30, 88–90, 124–27
    and prioritization, 1–3, 25–29, 59–61, 101–2, 136–39, 140–44
    and reinforcement, 28–29, 33–40, 59–63, 145–49
    as rhythm, 23–25, 31, 109–10
    metrics vs. messages, 28–29
    resolving what matters, 59–61, 140–44
    "vision leaks" and repetition, 31, 80–82
    See also "Resolve What Matters" rhythm
click track metaphor, 17–19
coherence
    coherent answers to employee questions, 6, 43–44, 115–19
    coherent systems vs. heroic effort, 12–13, 39–40, 52–53, 57–60
communication
    limits of engagement programs, 5–6, 83–86, 111–14
    more information vs. clarity, 25–27
    messaging vs. mechanics, 5–6, 10–11, 25–27, 57–60, 83–86, 99–103
compensation (people compensating for systems)
    absorbing friction, 10–13, 14–16, 49–53, 83–86, 94–97
    default stabilizers and heroes, 15–16, 52–53, 95–97, 158–61
    engagement vs. compensation, 5–7, 10–13, 83–86, 111–14
completion
    completion integrity pattern, 90–94, 154–57
    open loops and cognitive load, 49–52, 90–94, 154–57
    defining "done," 92–93, 154–57
    finishing vs. perpetual motion, 49–52, 90–94, 154–57
confidence
    in decisions and systems, 2–4, 14–16, 25–30, 58–60, 88–90, 102–3
    in future and growth, 44–45, 115–19
connection
    answers different question than clarity, 41–43
    and discretionary effort, 41–47, 69–71, 150–53
    disconnection and quiet withdrawal, 44–45
    invisible essential work, 41–47, 69–71, 150–53
    recognition mechanisms, 46–47, 69–71, 121–23, 150–53
    shared vs. leader-dependent connection, 46–48, 69–71
    See also Legacy Checks; "You Belong Here" rhythm
constraints and boundaries
    design vs. personal willpower, 49–53, 71–76, 158–61
    leadership as constraint-setting, 57–60, 59–63, 140–44
culture
    emerges from what is rewarded, ignored, excused, x, 1–4, 24, 28–29, 33–40
    scaling owner's mindset, 35–38
    training vs. daily reinforcement, x, 24, 33–40
customer experience
    employer promises and customer outcomes, 7–8, 11–13, 46–47, 105–7
    metrics teaching priorities, 3–4, 10–13, 28–29

INDEX

D

data and measurement
    effort vs. outcomes, 83–86, 111–14
    experience data vs. performance data, 77–79, 83–86, 111–14
    early indicators vs. lagging indicators, 52–53, 77–79, 83–87, 169

decision friction
    as early pattern, 86–90, 124–27, 158–61
    classification and durability, 88–90
    escalation and recycling, 87–88, 89–90
    restoring confidence, 88–90

decision-making
    clarity of ownership and boundaries, 29–30, 59–63, 88–90, 124–27
    speed vs. quality, 7–8, 52–53, 63–67, 88–90
    trade-offs and standards, 35–37, 59–63, 63–67, 140–44

design, structural
    design vs. intervention, 8, 12–13, 17–19, 57–60, 95–97, 162–68
    operating system concept, xii–xiii, 17–23, 57–60, 83–86, 109–10
    redesign for recovery, 49–53, 71–76, 152–53, 158–61

discretion vs. judgment, 2, 14–16, 25–30, 40, 44–45, 83–87

drift
    definition and predictability, xi, 6–8, 31, 82–83
    leadership blind spot and drift, 2–4, 58–60, 83–86

E

effort
    effort vs. energy, 13–16, 49–53, 83–86
    effort vs. impact, 6–7, 54, 83–85, 94, 98
    effort concentration pattern, 94–97, 158–61
    visible effort vs. quality of effort, 6–7, 13–16, 44–45, 83–86, 94–97

EFT (effort concentration heatmap), 158–61

emotional labor and leadership, 12–13, 21–23, 54–55, 72–76

engagement
    conditions vs. meaning, 5–7, 41–47, 111–14
    employee questions framework, 6, 43–44, 115–19
    job satisfaction vs. engagement, 5–7, 83–86, 111–14
    quiet disengagement, 6–7, 44–45, 95–97
    See also satisfaction

ESG of work (effort, strain, growth), 83–87, 115–19

exceptions
    naming vs. silent exceptions, 63–67, 145–49
    impact on standards, 35–37, 63–67, 145–49

experience, work. See work experience

F

fear and psychological safety, 4–5, 44–45, 69–71, 77–79, 115–19

feedback
    listening vs. changing conditions, 5–6, 48, 77–79, 115–19
    loops and follow-through, 6–7, 48, 77–79, 98, 115–19

friction
    decision friction, 86–90, 124–27
    operational friction and effort, 10–13, 25–27, 83–87, 124–27
    structural vs. personal, 10–13, 14–16, 49–53, 83–87

G

growth (employee)
    as engagement driver, 43–45, 115–19
    plateaus and stalled growth, 44–45, 115–19

H

habits and routines
    accidental rhythms, 20–22, 59–60, 80–82
    rehearsal and preparation, 17–19, 35–38, 121–23

heroes and heroics
    hero-based systems vs. design-based systems, 12–13, 39–40, 52–53, 95–97, 158–61

leadership heroics vs. operating system, xii–xiii, 8, 57–60, 80–82
Hershey Entertainment & Resorts
  Legacy Check program, 46–47, 121–23
  values: Own, Anticipate, Delight, Inspire, 46–47, 121–23
  hiring and onboarding
  unspoken realities, 10–13, 115–19
  promises vs. tools and systems, 10–13

I

identity (organizational)
  formed through repetition, 33–35
  patterns vs. intent, 33–40, 58–60, 109–10
  recognizable identity, 40, 58–60
implementation vs. intention, 24–25, 35–40, 57–60, 99–103
intentionality
  consistency vs. perfection, 33–35, 39–40, 63–67
  everyday trade-offs, 35–37, 63–67, 145–49
  reinforcement discipline, 33–40, 63–67, 145–49
  See also "Hold the Line" rhythm
interpretation cost
  interpreting expectations, 1–3, 25–27, 31, 83–87, 108
  interpreting mottos vs. mechanics, 5–6, 24–25, 57–60, 99–103
invisible work
  behind-the-scenes contributions, 41–47, 69–71, 150–53
  success defined by absence of failure, 69–71, 150–53

J

judgment
  judgment vs. rules and scripts, 2, 14–16, 25–30, 49–53, 83–87
  preserved by recovery, 14–16, 54–55, 71–76, 109–10
  supported by clarity and intentionality, 25–31, 33–40, 58–60

K

Kahn, William A., 42, 112, 169
knowledge, institutional, 7–8, 94–97

L

Legacy Checks (Hershey)
  design mechanics, 46–47, 121–23
  values linkage, 46–47, 121–23
  visibility and social reinforcement, 46–47, 121–23
leadership
  as design role, 57–60, 58–63, 162–68
  as pattern ownership, 58–60, 80–82
  blind spot on alignment, 2–4, 10–13, 58–60, 83–86
  non-delegable pattern decisions, 58–60, 59–82
  presence vs. design, 37–40, 58–60, 80–82
listening
  employee questions and listening, 6, 115–19
  hearing the system, 76–79, 83–87, 169
Locke, Edwin A., 111–12, 169

M

meaning and purpose
  erosion of meaning, 1–3, xi, 6–8, 17–21
  making meaning visible, 25–31, 41–47, 109–10
measurement
  business outcomes vs. experience, 83–86, 111–14, 169
  decision friction, completion, effort concentration, 86–98, 124–27, 154–61
  hearing the system rhythm, 76–79, 83–87, 109–10
  recovery experience research, 52–53, 169
mechanisms
  Legacy Checks as mechanism, 46–47, 121–23
  recognition and reinforcement mechanisms, 46–47, 69–71, 121–23, 150–53
  RHYTHM tools as mechanisms, 108–10, 136–68
meetings
  where clarity breaks, 60–61, 140–44
  recurring forums and rhythms, 20–22, 59–61, 80–82, 162–68
mindset vs. system design, 11–16, 49–53, 111–14

N

noise and instability, 10–13, 49–53, 83–87

O

operating system, leadership
    definition, xii–xiii, 17–23, 57–60, 83–86, 109–10
    leadership OS vs. accidental patterns, 17–23, 58–60, 80–82

ownership
    decision and work ownership, 29–30, 94–97, 154–57
    personal ownership vs. system responsibility, 8, 15–16, 49–53, 57–60

P

pace and tempo
    always-on work, 49–52, 71–76
    occupancy and micro-recovery, 74–76

pacing demand, 49–53, 71–76, 162–68

patterns
    accidental rhythms, 20–22, 59–60
    behavior patterns vs. messages, 3–4, 19–22, 33–40, 58–60

pattern decisions in RHYTHM, 59–82

performance
    activity vs. impact, 6–7, 54, 83–85, 94, 98

performance data and engagement, 7–8, 83–86, 111–14

performance vs. behavior standards, 63–67, 145–49

pressure
    under pressure tests of standards, 7–8, 35–37, 52–53, 63–67, 140–44
    response to pressure and rhythm, 17–23, 49–55, 71–76

priorities
    conflicting priorities, 1–3, 25–29, 59–61, 101–2, 136–39, 140–44
    protected vs. variable commitments, 59–61, 140–44
    what breaks first map, 59–61, 140–44

promises
    brand and employer promises, x, 7–8, 11–13, 105–7
    promises vs. discipline, 7–8, 33–40, 57–60, 105–7

purpose
    breaking under pressure, xi–xii, 6–8, 17–23, 54–55, 99–103

purpose and rhythm, 17–23, 54–55, 109–10

purpose vs. survival, 99–100
    turning words into work, 57–60, 83–87, 99–103

Q

questions, key
    four employee questions, 6, 43–44, 115–19
    leadership repeat questions, 62–63, 66–67, 71–72, 76–77, 81–82, 101–2, 130–31, 162–68
    "How will you know it when you see it?", 25–26, 31, 136–39

R

ratings and scales
    rating scales explained, 135
    purpose reality check scale, 136–39

recognition
    specific vs. generic praise, 46–47, 69–71, 121–23, 150–53
    tied to values and contributions, 41–47, 69–71, 121–23, 150–53
    visibility and social recognition, 46–47, 150–53

recovery
    recovery as structural, 49–53, 71–76, 109–10
    recovery experience research, 52–53, 169
    recovery inside work vs. outside work, 49–53, 71–76
    See also "Tempo the Work" rhythm

relationships and attention
    predictable leadership attention, 47–48, 69–71, 115–19
    attention only during crisis, 47–48, 77–79, 145–49

resilience
    limits of resilience without design, 15–16, 49–53
    mislabeling structural problems as resilience gaps, 49–53, 83–87

resources and capacity
    capacity constraints and trade-offs, 7–8, 59–61, 71–76, 140–44
    stabilizers and over-reliance, 15–16, 95–97, 158–61
responsibility
    leadership responsibility for patterns, 58–60, 81–82, 102–3
    personal vs. system responsibility, 10–13, 15–16, 49–53, 57–60
rework and repetition
    rework as signal, 7–8, 77–79, 86–87, 90–94
    repetition and identity, 17–23, 33–35, 80–82, 109–10
RHYTHM Operating System
    definition and loop, xii–xiv, 17–23, 109–10
    elements overview, xiii–xiv, 59–82, 109–10
    practical tools, 108–10, 124–68
    resolving failures in RHYTHM, 54–55, 109–10

S

safety, psychological. See belonging; connection
satisfaction vs. engagement
    definitions and research, 5–7, 83–86, 111–14, 169
    leadership mistakes, 5–7, 111–14
satisfaction as floor, engagement as ceiling, 114
Schein, Edgar H., 33, 169
self-protection
    defensive pacing and hedging, xi, 4–5, 6–7, 15–16, 44–45, 52–53, 83–86
    rational disengagement, 6–7, 44–45, 99–100
signals and cues
    metrics and placement, 3–4, 10–13, 28–29
signals of strain, 49–53, 76–79, 83–87, 136–39
Silver Diner, 105–7
standards
    reinforcing standards under pressure, 33–40, 63–67, 145–49

owners' standards (Half Day Cafe), 35–38
standards vs. convenience, 35–37, 63–67, 145–49
strain and friction
    workarounds as signal, 10–13, 76–79, 83–87, 95–97
system strain vs. individual stress, 14–16, 49–53, 83–87
surveys
    limits of engagement surveys, 5–6, 83–86, 135
    when leaders are already late, 6–7, 119–20

T

tempo. See pace and tempo; "Tempo the Work" rhythm
trade-offs
    making trade-offs visible, 35–37, 59–63, 140–44
    what breaks first map, 59–61, 140–44
trust
    erosion of trust in reliability, 7–8, 25–30, 33–40, 63–67, 83–87
    rebuilding through consistency, 33–40, 63–67, 80–82, 102–3

U

urgency
    constant urgency and depletion, 49–52, 71–76
    vague urgency vs. prioritization, 25–27, 60–61, 73–74
utility of programs vs. design, 5–6, 10–13, 49–53, 83–87, 108–10

V

values
    explicit vs. lived values, x, 24, 28–29, 33–40, 145–49
    Hershey values (Own, Anticipate, Delight, Inspire), 46–47, 121–23
values as lenses for recognition, 46–47, 121–23
visibility
    contribution visibility map, 150–53
    visibility of effort and standards, 28–29, 41–47, 69–71, 121–23, 150–53

W

Weick, Karl E., 25, 169
work design
    work as recoverable or depleting, 49–53, 71–76, 109–10
    work teaching priorities, 2–4, 19–22, 24, 28–29, 33–40, 57–60
work experience
    felt experience vs. outcomes, 2–4, 6–7, 41–47, 83–87
    measuring what work actually feels like, 76–79, 83–98, 136–39
workload
    reasonable workload and boundaries, 15–16, 49–53, 71–76
    demand vs. capacity, 59–61, 71–76, 140–44
workflows and systems
    core systems and misalignment, 10–13, 49–53, 83–87
    accidental vs. designed workflows, 20–22, 57–60, 83–87

Y

"You Belong Here" rhythm
    defining meaningful contribution, xiii–xiv, 41–47, 67–71, 109–10
    reducing replaceability, 41–47, 67–71, 150–53
    visibility of contributions, 41–47, 69–71, 121–23, 150–53

www.ingramcontent.com/pod-product-compliance
Lightning Source LLC
LaVergne TN
LVHW061612070526
838199LV00078B/7255